The John Fresolo Saga

The John Fresolo Saga

*Political Conspiracy Exposed
in the Massachusetts State House*

By Richard F. Wright

NEB Publishing

London ^ Jefferson MA USA ^ Melbourne

The John Fresolo Saga

Political Conspiracy Exposed
in the Massachusetts State House

ISBN 978-1-7340081-0-4

Library of Congress Control Number: 2019913525

First Edition – October 2019

10 9 8 7 6 5 4 3 2 1

Printed in the United States

Book Cover Design by Sarah Conti

The Books of Richard F Wright

http://richard-wright.blogspot.com

Contents

"No member or officer of the House of Representatives
pressured John Fresolo to resign, said Seth Gitell,
spokesperson for House Speaker Robert A. DeLeo."

Michael Levenson, *Boston Globe*, May 22, 2013

Introduction

U ntil now, it remained a mystery to the thousands of voters in the 16th Worcester District why their State Representative suddenly resigned in 2013. He had just won reelection to his eighth term, in a race where he was unopposed, and where polling data showed his popularity and voter approval had never been higher. In fact, polling data showed that he was popular enough to make a run for State Senator if he was inclined.

The shocking truth as to his decision to resign was not about the allegations brought against him by his office aide, rather by the strategic conspiracy by State House Leadership to rid themselves of a pesky non-conformist in their midst.

My investigation presented here in *The John Fresolo Saga, Political Conspiracy Exposed in the Massachusetts State House*, reveals that the vague and salacious allegations made against John Fresolo provided the launching pad for those who personally and professionally despised Fresolo to pressure him into a much-regretted resignation.

After months of accusation, speculation, and lascivious media coverage, the tedious, plodding investigation process had reached a point where the ethics committee members were ready to exact an apology, and some contrition from the Representative and perhaps a censure for ethical excesses. But then, the agreement-nearly-in-hand was overturned by the State House Leadership, and Fresolo faced an impossible situation, ultimately resigning to protect a large number of innocent people. It was a decision he came to regret.

The thousands of voters who had returned John Fresolo to elected office for the eighth straight term were denied his leadership, devotion, and dedication just when his seniority was reaching a point that could have had a significant impact for his district.

The untold story is now revealed in all its grittiness as those who sought to throw John Fresolo out of the House used every pressure tactic known to bury him. My investigation was a two-year effort that included hundreds of hours of face-to-face and telephone interviews, review and interpretation of letters, emails, documents, daily journals, hearing exhibits, testimony notes, and media reports. Exact quotations have been drawn from interviews, meeting notes, journals, and other documents. Representative John Fresolo also agreed to answer questions in a series of face-to-face interviews and agreed to have no editorial control over my manuscript.

The saga is tracked chronologically from the day in late November 2012 when Jamie Ryan, Fresolo's administrative aide, accidentally uncovers a photograph not intended for her to see until Fresolo resigns six months later.

In an unmistakable rush to judgment, from the moment that the claimant, Ryan, showed the lawyers in the State House a photo of John Fresolo's genitals until he resigned, it was only 69 days; sixty-nine days filled with false allegations, a kangaroo court proceeding, and an ugly conspiracy fueled by fear, hatred, and arrogance.

For all the state and local public officials who called for the investigation material to be released; for the members of the media including reporters, columnists, radio and TV talk-show hosts in Worcester and Boston and various bloggers who all called for the investigation materials to be released; here it is.

It may be John Fresolo's saga, but it's the voters of his district and voters everywhere in the State who have been abused.

Richard F. Wright
Jefferson, Mass.
October 2019

Richard F. Wright

Part One – Allegations

al-le-ga-tion

noun

Plural noun: allegations

- a claim or assertion that someone has done something illegal or wrong, typically one made without proof.

Richard F. Wright

Chapter One

The Accuser – Jamie Ryan

Tuesday, November 20, 2012

Upon returning to her office at the Massachusetts State House following her honeymoon, Jamie Ryan went about her tasks intending to catch up first on voice mail messages and email messages that she would have to review and answer for the Representative. As she reported later to the House Counsel, she checked on the Facebook account too as there may be items to read and the Rep may have left some items for her to upload as she usually did.

Ryan was thrilled that her boss, Representative John Fresolo, of Worcester, had attended her wedding reception. He had agreed, although at first reluctantly, to drive to Rhode Island and spend a few short hours before driving home to Worcester in anticipation of attending one of his two annual fundraising rallies early the next morning. He had tried to plead out of attending his Legislative Aide's wedding because he would be too exhausted to attend and manage his own important event the next day.

But, ultimately, mainly when he detected her weeping eyes, of which she was admittedly somewhat infamous, he relented. On his arrival, Ryan was happy to introduce him around and especially to the supporters of Congressman Steve Lynch of the 8th Congressional District. She was thrilled when the conservative Fresolo acknowledged that he was supporting Steve Lynch for US Senate.

Ryan had many reasons to be happy. She was just married, she was on a career path that kept her close to the political mainstream, and as she had been heard to say, "I was born to be in the State House." As a Legislative Aide in the House of Representatives, she was near the heartbeat of Massachusetts politics, right where she wanted to be.

Fresolo had enough reasons to be happy too as he had just won reelection running unopposed in a district that he had represented for eight consecutive terms. The somewhat gritty urban southeast side of Worcester suited the slightly gritty persona that John Fresolo presented to the outside world. He was always prepared to fight for his constituents, even to the point of exerting effort beyond what they expected. His supporters were true loyalists. He was loyal to his district, and his district was loyal to him. His popularity had never been higher.

Fresolo had asked Ryan to update some information on pending legislation, and she decided to look back at prior emails to find the information. As Ryan went about checking, she came upon a message that had a photograph of a flaccid penis. It was a close-up image without any background to show who it was or where the photo had been taken. It startled her to see it. She closed it immediately.

Months later in an interview with attorneys in the Office of Legal Counsel, she admitted that she realized the image had not been sent to her, but was in fact, sent to a different person by the Representative. She admitted that she showed the image to a co-worker and eventually to others, but that she didn't take any action or make any comment about it to her boss at the time. In testimony during a hearing the following spring, it was admitted by her co-worker that they had viewed the image together with "derisive amusement." It was true Ryan had been startled seeing the image but that she did not become physically sick or have an unreasonable emotional breakdown, or want to vomit, having seen it. They had giggled and dismissed it.

Her co-worker advised her at the time of first discovering the photograph that if she was going to seek to get a different assignment in the State House, as they had previously been discussing, she shouldn't mention the picture or any of the messages they had read when she contacted the Human Resources (HR) department. In Ryan's mind, she was just seeking how to move on to an assignment with more advancement opportunities and better benefits, such as paid maternity leave. She planned to visit the HR department as soon as possible.

It was Thanksgiving week, and Ryan was pleased that the Representative had given her the day after Thanksgiving off. This would be her first Thanksgiving with her new husband, and this would be a wonderful weekend.

Tuesday, November 27, 2012

The Representative tried to reach Ryan on the telephone but failed to contact her after making four attempts. When he finally did reach her, he confronted her about being away from her desk. Ryan felt his anger about not being accessible, and it contributed further to her desire to leave her job and find another one in the State House.

At one point during the day, Ryan spoke with a co-worker who had an office near hers. Ryan expressed her concerns about the way the Representative had spoken to her about being absent from her desk. And, she spontaneously told her friend about finding the picture on the Representative's computer. They discussed Ryan's desire to leave her current job and find another. Her friend counseled her to go to HR and see what she could find. She suggested that she not mention the picture to HR.

The next day, Ryan went to HR and tried to learn how to make a transfer to a different job. She did not mention the photograph, and she tried to find out if she could request a transfer and *not* notify her boss. The HR department personnel told her there would be lots of job openings when the new term started in January and that she should look then.

Thursday, November 29, 2012

Ryan finally decided to see if there was a way to get a transfer and not end up in a confrontation with her boss about leaving. She called the Office of Legal Counsel to see if they could give her some advice.

Dana Fleming, Deputy Counsel in the Office of Legal Counsel, returned Ryan's call.

"Jamie, this is Dana Fleming, in the House Counsel office. I'm calling in response to your inquiry to our office. How can I help you?"

"I want to transfer out of my current position with Representative Fresolo to another position in the House."

"Is there a specific reason why you want a transfer?"

"I had contacted HR (Human Resources) and spoke to Keith Johnson, and he told me that I should wait until February when new positions may open up."

"That's the right thing to do. HR will have notices of openings, and you can then interview for them."

"I want to transfer without letting the Rep know I'm doing it."

"Is there any particular reason why you don't want the Representative to know you are seeking a transfer. Staff do apply for open positions and movements are made."

"I really don't want to go into that. I don't know you well enough and don't trust you enough, to go into it. I just want to find a new position without my boss finding out about it."

"I'm afraid that I couldn't guarantee total anonymity during the search process. But you should tell me if you felt you were being retaliated against or otherwise mistreated by Fresolo or anyone else."

"I just don't know you or trust you enough to say more."

"I understand. I want to assure you we want to help, but we can't help you if you don't tell us what your concerns are or what is wrong. We will do our very best to keep any information confidential, and I want you to know that I have had experience handling personnel matters, including sexual harassment complaints."

"I don't know. I'm just not sure I can trust anyone."

"Let's leave it at this. You should call back at any time if you feel like talking. We are ready to help."

It would be three months later before Ryan re-contacted the Office of Legal Counsel about getting a job transfer.

Tuesday, March 5, 2013 (three months later)

On Tuesday, March 5, 2013, Ryan determined that she would call the Office of Legal Counsel and arrange to talk to someone about questions she had in her mind about the new ethics advisory and how it affected her job as an aide to State Representative Fresolo. The advisory had revised and clarified instructions on what the legislators were permitted to do when making personal recommendations on behalf of job applicants.

Ryan dialed the Office of Legal Counsel, and her message was sent to Chief Legal Counsel James C. Kennedy. When Kennedy got the inquiry, he directed his assistant, Deputy Chief Legal Counsel Dana Fleming, to respond to Ryan.

Fleming telephoned Ryan that morning and had a conversation with her about the ethics advisory. Ryan asked a few questions, and Fleming answered the best she could. As the discussion concluded, Ryan asked if she could meet, in person, with Fleming to discuss some concerns she had about the conduct of her boss, Representative Fresolo. Fleming agreed they could meet, and they set a time for later that day.

According to notes Fleming kept of the meeting, Ryan became visibly upset as soon as they got together.

Ryan said, "I want to know if I can get a transfer out of Rep Fresolo's office? I have an interview for another position within the House scheduled for tomorrow," she added.

Fleming asked, "Why did you want to speak in private?

"Representative Fresolo used his state email account to send sexual and dirty pictures to someone, which had made me want to vomit."

Ryan made a point to explain to Fleming, "I don't want to get the representative in trouble. I don't want to be perceived as a snitch, and I really want to remain anonymous," she added. "Also, I'm afraid that by complaining or asking to transfer that I may lose my job and ruin my reputation."

Fleming spoke right up to assure Ryan that she had nothing to fear.

"The Office of Legal Counsel will do everything in its power to keep your identity confidential, but these allegations are serious enough to warrant further investigation and need to be shared with others on a need-to-know basis."

The two agreed to meet the next day, Wednesday, although there was concern over the large snowstorm that was making its way to New England. When the meeting started, Fleming asked for more detail about the photograph.

Ryan said, "It's a picture of the representative's genitals, which he apparently sent to a woman named, (Jane Doe)[1], in November 2012 using his House email account."

---

[1] This is the only pseudonym used to maintain privacy

Fleming asked if Ryan still had a copy of the email and photograph?

Ryan said, "I still have it."

"I told Associate Legal Counsel Iannuccillo about the photograph when I first discovered it in November 2012."

Fleming said to Ryan, "I recall Counsel (Iannuccillo) mentioning it at the time, but he only indicated it was a personnel matter and did not give details that included the existence of the photograph. If I had been aware of these allegations at the time, I would have addressed them with you," she added.

Fleming said to Ryan, "I have checked the records on this; you and I spoke on Thursday, November 29, 2012. I asked you several questions, and you declined to be specific. You told me you didn't know me and didn't trust me. You refused to give details about your concern. You said all I want is to look for a different position."

During that telephone call in November, Fleming attempted to explain that she could not help Ryan if she did not know what was wrong. At the time, Fleming said to Ryan, "I will do my very best to keep the information confidential." One final time Ryan said she didn't know, or trust Fleming and the conversation concluded by Fleming indicating that Ryan could call back any time.

"I can give you a copy of the photograph if you want it," said Ryan. "I have only told one other House employee about the photograph. Do you want me to bring in a copy?"

Fleming responded, "Yes, bring it in tomorrow." Ryan then took the time to explain to Fleming that the Representative had never sexually harassed her, other than occasionally calling her "hon" or "sweetie," which she found annoying, but not offensive.

Thursday, March 7, 2013

On Thursday, March 7, 2013, Fleming contacted Ryan by phone to offer her an opportunity to "go on paid administrative leave until the allegations could be resolved."

Ryan had elected to work from home due to the weather and was not able to bring in the photograph. Ryan said to Fleming, "I don't want to go on paid administrative leave. I want to remain anonymous in this and paid leave would raise a lot of questions."

Fleming explained, "It's likely the Representative would eventually learn of the allegations and that the Office of Legal Counsel could not guarantee complete anonymity."

"I don't want to go on paid administrative leave, and I don't want to leave my job unfinished," said Ryan.

Fleming changed the subject and asked again about the photograph.

Fleming asked Ryan, "Are you willing to bring in the photograph?"

Ryan "reluctantly" agreed. She added, "I don't want to get the Representative in trouble."

Fleming said, "Jamie, I understand, but now that the allegations had been brought to our attention, we will need to investigate further."

Ryan was distressed at this response.

Fleming continued, "Getting you a new position is our first priority, but I must consider how to improve the environment for the next aide who would fill your shoes."

Ryan responded, "Maybe representative Fresolo might be better off with a male aide."

Friday, March 8, 2013

On Friday, March 8, the city was digging out from under the recent snowstorm. Ryan came into Fleming's office at 9:30 AM with photocopies in a manila envelope. It was still snowing out, and Ryan indicated to Fleming that bringing in the photograph was the only reason she came in today. Fleming did not rush Ryan. They talked for a while.

Ryan asked, "Will I be able to go on paid administrative leave now?"

Fleming said, "Yes, just as we discussed yesterday. When would you want to have the paid leave start," she added?

"I would like to start today – but I don't know what I would tell Representative Fresolo."

Fleming said, "Let's agree that you will tell him you are going home sick and you will need not mention the paid administrative leave to the Representative. The Office of Legal Counsel will take care of that," she added.

Becoming visibly shaken, Ryan thanked Fleming. Ryan said, "I'm still concerned about my job security."

Fleming said, "As I wrote to you in the email on March 7, it is the policy of the House not to retaliate against individuals who come forward with complaints."

Perking up, Ryan asked, "Where would my new position be?"

Fleming said she didn't know.

Ryan said, "You know, I had an interview for a researcher position on the House side of a Joint Committee, but I think representative Fresolo probably didn't do me any favors getting that job."

Fleming was confused by the comment. "What do you mean he didn't do you any favors?"

Ryan said, "I think Representative Fresolo had probably told the Chairman that he didn't want me to get the job because then he would have to find a new aide. Now, I don't have any information to support that, other than the fact that the Chairman told me the committee received several qualified applicants."

Fleming said, "Let's let the hiring process play out before jumping to any conclusions. You haven't *not* gotten the job yet, so let's see what happens, and then we can take whatever steps we need to take from there." Ryan agreed.

"Actually, I prefer any job that accrues time, not like a Legislative Aide position, so that I can have a paid maternity leave someday. My husband and I want to start a family. I would be a good researcher because I know I would be good at that type of job."

Fleming told Ryan, "I can't promise any specific position, but I will certainly relay your preferences and see whether or not they could be accommodated."

Fleming went on to remind Ryan that she would not be retaliated against and that the House would find her another position somewhere in the organization.

Ryan said, "Could I get that in writing from you?"

Fleming said, "I need to get permission to send something like that to you, but I'm sure I can probably do it."

Fleming had been patient with Ryan on these various matters as it was clear that Ryan was not enthusiastic about revealing the contents of the manila envelope. Having covered a wide range of issues to Ryan's satisfaction, Ryan finally showed a photocopy of the picture to Fleming. The photograph was a close-up picture of a flaccid penis. The Representative's face is not in the picture. The date on the document was November 15, 2012, and it was addressed to (Jane Doe).

Ryan also gave Fleming a photocopy of the Facebook page message, which included several message boxes at the bottom. On the photocopy, one of the boxes has suggestive language that reads: "I miss licking you." Another message states: "I'm with the John now, so that won't work."

As Ryan showed the page to Attorney Fleming, she said, "This message is highly suggestive that the representative was communicating with a prostitute over his Facebook account."

Fleming was not sure that was the correct interpretation of the message, but let it go.

Note: It was later determined by the Office of Legal Counsel that the person addressed in the message had a family member named John. The inference drawn by Ryan of a prostitute was incorrect.)

Ryan described to Fleming that the Representative instructs her to update his Facebook page routinely.

"I see these types of messages routinely, and sometimes I even respond to the women informing them that they haven't reached the representative but rather have reached his aide."

Fleming asked, "Have any of the women you wrote to ever wrote back?"

Ryan said, "Yes, sometimes they write oops or sorry."

Ryan described to Fleming that the representative used his personal Facebook account for political purposes and logs on to his Facebook page using his House of Representatives provided email account. She described that was how she accessed his Facebook page for him.

Fleming probed further with Ryan to determine if there were other issues she wanted to share. During an extended back and forth, Ryan ticked off several things that the Representative asked her to do that she was not happy about. She expressed concern about the Representative's other aide with whom she claimed she had no contact. Ryan also pointed out that the Representative had her make phone calls when his sister was facing jury duty, helping his daughter with a college application, calling employers on behalf of job seekers, and asking her to help with campaign duties. Fleming made careful notes on these topics and collected as much detail as she could from Ryan. In all, Fleming now had seven complaints attributed to Ryan.

Ryan returned to the subject of her job security and said, "I don't just want to be stuck somewhere so that someone is forced to add me to their staff. You know what I'm referring to, they are known in the House as *Speaker Specials*[2]. These are jobs the Speaker gets for people to be placed somewhere just because the Speaker says so."

Fleming said she was not aware of those jobs, and that would not be the case for Ryan. Fleming said, "I can't promise you any particular position, but the House would do its best to find a good fit."

Ryan asked, "Would I need to interview for the position?"

Fleming said, "It's entirely possible an interview would be required, but again, I can't say with any certainty at this point."

Fleming said, "Jamie, let's take a step back and focus on the first things first, which means parting ways with the Representative and going on paid leave. Also, will you need any help taking things home today or finishing up your work for the day?"

Ryan said, "No, there is only one work assignment to finish up, and I brought bags to take home my personal things; I should be all set." The meeting concluded, and Ryan left.

Ryan had successfully found a way to leave her job in Fresolo's office and to move on to another position in the State House, perhaps one with opportunities for advancement and benefits. Her allegations that the Representative was using State House computers for sexually inappropriate contact with people had sparked a vigorous reaction from Fleming, someone who had many years of prior experience working on behalf of women who had been sexually harassed in the

---

[2] Speaker Specials refer to a position forced onto someone's State House staff

workplace. Fleming was now ready to help launch a thorough investigation of Fresolo and what else he might be doing.

Richard F. Wright

Chapter Two

The Accused – John Fresolo

Friday, March 8, 2013

Jim Kennedy made the call he didn't want to make.

It was early evening on a Friday, and he had to call the Representative at home now – or wait until Monday. The written order from House Speaker Robert DeLeo was hand-delivered to him minutes ago. Waiting until Monday would keep the knot that had been developing in Jim's stomach all day for another two days and let the Rep have one last weekend of peace.

Kennedy decided to pass the stomach knot on to the unsuspecting Rep. He dialed the Rep's cell phone.

"I'm sorry to disturb you at home, John, but the Office of Legal Counsel had received several complaints from your aide, Jamie Ryan," said Kennedy.

Kennedy, Chief Legal Counsel, explained to Fresolo that his aide had contacted them to launch complaints against him and that the Speaker of the House had ordered his office to investigate the complaints.

"I'm calling you to notify you of the complaints," said Kennedy. He further explained that Ryan had been placed on paid administrative leave at the State House and would not be returning to work in the Representative's office on March 11, 2013.

Kennedy told John that once anyone comes to the Office of Legal Counsel with complaints, "We have an ethical obligation to the institution and as an attorney, to look into it."

Kennedy continued, "I apologize for calling so late on a Friday night, but I thought you would want to know about the allegations."

Fresolo was incredulous, "What are the allegations, what could they possibly be?"

Kennedy responded, "There are seven complaints. First that you used your House email account to send out inappropriate images of your anatomy and second, that you had accessed your Facebook page through your House email account to send sexually explicit messages."

Fresolo's mind raced. While Kennedy was talking his brain was asking – *You thought I would want to know about the allegations? Who would want to hear something like that at any time?*

His mind continued racing. How could he counter these charges, how could he keep it quiet, how could he fix whatever was broken for Ryan that would drive her to make allegations like this? He couldn't focus on what Kennedy was saying.

The emotional meltdown that he experienced that night exceeded any he had previously endured. Not a stranger to controversy, political brawling, and public humiliation over a messy divorce, the nature of these charges from his aide was beyond anything he had weathered before.

As Kennedy continued to lay out the specific details of the charges during the phone call, John slipped into his defensive posture, of which he was famous, to take each allegation and dismiss it on the spot with Kennedy. Kennedy was not open to hearing a defense against the charges. His job was to alert the Representative and give him some specific instructions.

First, John was not to expect his aide to show up for work on Monday. She was gone, and she was going to be transferred to another job at the State House.

"I'm calling you to alert you to the fact that she has been placed on administrative leave."

Kennedy stated that his office would begin the investigation next week.

"Given that the allegations are pending, you should have no further contact with Jamie."

At this point, John had been standing in his kitchen, clutching his cell phone to his ear for 10 minutes, and his mind was racing. Doesn't Jim realize that there must be something wrong with Ryan? John felt he's treated her fairly as an employee. Didn't he even go out of his way recently to attend her wedding when it was a major conflict with other personal plans? Who else would do that for his aide? Then Kennedy's voice broke through.

"John, this is an internal investigation and only seven people know about the complaint at this point, me, Deputy

Counsel Dana Fleming, Speaker DeLeo, Jim Eisenberg, the Speaker's chief of staff, Toby Morelli, the Speaker's deputy chief of staff, your aide Jamie, and now finally, you."

Seven people now knew that his aide of the past two years was making allegations that John's genitalia was exposed on Facebook?

"For crying out loud, Jim, I don't even know how to use Facebook!"

Fresolo explained to Kennedy that he doesn't use Facebook, doesn't know his own password, that's something he gave to his aide for her to use, and how could any picture get there unless she put it there?

"She's the only one who knows the password!"

"John, I will do everything in my power to keep the investigation confidential," said Kennedy.

"I'm worried about the fact that the Speaker, Eisenberg, and Morelli all know about the complaint. Even though I haven't done anything to hurt those three, they still treat me terribly."

"John, you can trust leadership to keep this information confidential."

Kennedy listened to some more of Fresolo's exasperation.

"I'm stunned by these allegations. It's mind-boggling what she's saying. Jim, you must know I'm not computer literate. I don't know how to do all that stuff. If I sent a picture through my phone, I don't understand why it would be on the computer? I had no idea any images would be transmitted using my House email account."

"I understand," said Kennedy. "But once someone comes to the Office of Legal Counsel with a complaint, I have an ethical obligation as an attorney and to the institution to look into it."

"Jim, I have never done anything to hurt people. Any picture that I sent was from a phone text, not the House computer."

"We will investigate all these issues, and I have no reason to disbelieve you, but if you have a phone that is synced with your House email account, the picture would have come from that account,"

"Jim, I have always been good to my aide, and I don't understand why she is trying to hurt me, or why she is doing this?

Reeling from the realization of how serious these charges were, John sputtered to Kennedy, "I have never done anything to hurt people and that the picture was sent from my phone, if I sent a picture from my phone, all I can do is apologize for sending the photos. I regret taking that picture and sending it. It only happened that one time. I had no knowledge that pictures sent on the phone would go through the State House email system."

Kennedy offered what little support he could by indicating that the matter would stay confidential for the time being.

"I have never experienced a confidential communication that did not stay confidential in the Speaker's office. I have worked in the building long enough to appreciate that an allegation does not have to be true to be harmful. We are all taking the matter very seriously, and we understand the potential stakes involved," added Kennedy.

Fresolo had paced two miles in his small kitchen and in the past 20 minutes trying to piece together how this situation erupted, where he could turn for help, and wondering why was Ryan doing this now? Was it her desire to get a better job somewhere? He knew she had applied for another position, but that's not uncommon among young aides in the State House. Everyone knows John won't be getting a Chairmanship with the Speaker as an adversary, so an aide would likely want to move to a Representative with more upward mobility and broader coattails for a political or government career. He's got that clear, that's okay; that's no reason to torpedo your boss to get ahead. It's just not making sense.

"John, I'm sorry for calling this late, I weighed whether to call tonight or to wait until Monday, but I thought you might rather know sooner rather than later."

While John was churning his options to get help, to get answers, to get this nightmare cleared up, Kennedy was churning on about other allegations.

"John, there is a complaint that you have another aide that does not appear for work."

"What?"

"Jamie claims that she has never spoken to your other aide, Ken Simoncini."

"Listen, Ken is my district aide and has been for years. He takes care of things in my district.

"Ryan claims she has never spoken to or emailed him."

"That's simply not true. Just recently, she had to interact with him to come into Boston to attend an ethics training course. She arranged for a place for him to park his car, escorted him to the training area, of course, she knows him. He handles things in the district so she may not email him, but he usually handles things on the phone. It's nonsense that she doesn't know him."

"I understand, I'm just relaying the allegation that has been made by her. I have formed no opinion as to the veracity of the allegations, and we plan to do a full investigation. I hope you will trust us to do the job needed and that the truth will come out?"

"I do trust you and the Legal Office, but I believe Jamie is on a witch hunt and that she is sick and psychotic."

Fresolo, in his own mind, could only imagine that this was a deliberate act by Jamie to somehow damage him. He knew that he had never "placed" that message and photograph on an email, or on Facebook, or anything like that. He knew he had sent a text by cell phone, but how could they be related? Kennedy didn't seem to be listening to him.

Fresolo went on to explain, "It was just last week that Jamie advised me that she was interviewing for another job with another member. I told her I was fine with that and that I would never stand in her way of getting another position or bettering herself professionally."

"These claims Jamie has made are mind-boggling and frankly have tipped me upside down. I haven't done anything wrong, and I treat my aide with the utmost respect. I have never said anything inappropriate to her," John added.

Fresolo went on to describe that occasionally he brings in a former Representative from his district, John Rucho, and he sometimes makes comments, "about Jamie's weight, things like that."

"While I know those comments are inappropriate, I really can't stop him from making those comments as he's much older and from a different generation and less attuned to these sorts of things."

"John, we will sit down with your aide and hear her out and also sit down with you and hear your side of the story."

"Jim, there is no *side* to the story. There is no story."

"Let me stress that the Office of Legal Counsel has come to no conclusions, and we have formed no opinions about this matter. I'm only calling to make you aware of the allegations and to alert you to the fact that your aide has been placed on administrative leave. We will begin the investigation next week."

"Jim, I have never done anything intentionally, and I will make myself available as you want. This job is my entire livelihood, I have no other income."

As he said it, he realized how pathetic it must sound to Jim that he was pleading for his job. But it was true, he felt he worked all day every day for the voters in his district, even when they had a different interpretation of what state government should be doing compared to the current and previous leadership.

"Jim, I had no way to know that a picture from my phone would go through the State House system. It's a phone connection, wouldn't it just go to the other phone? All I can do is apologize."

Fresolo described his understanding of messages on Facebook as being private that they are only being sent to the person with whom he is talking.

Kennedy told Fresolo that given the allegations that are pending, he should have no further contact with Jamie.

"I've been nothing but a complete professional and a good boss toward Jamie, and I'm disappointed that she never brought any of this to my attention. I guess it would be difficult to continue working together under these circumstances."

"Jamie will be transferred to another position and is already on administrative leave."

"Jim, you know that I know Ryan was looking for another position. She had said she wanted a job where she could accrue time so that she could take a paid maternity leave because she wants to start a family. I didn't have a problem with her desire to look for another position. I just wish she had told me sooner because the session has started and I'm going to have to find a new aide."

Fresolo kept repeating that he couldn't believe this was happening.

"I ask Jamie to post pictures on Facebook for me all the time. I don't know how, and she handles that for me. I don't understand her. When she wants time off, I give it to her. Recently she helped me by drafting a resume for my daughter, and she told my daughter – your Dad is such a good boss."

Fresolo explained to Kennedy, "If I'm guilty of anything, it was certainly not intentional. I'm just blown away by these allegations."

"John, I understand. I'm empathetic, and if as you say you have done nothing wrong, then you should feel fine. But we will need to investigate this further. We will investigate the matter with all deliberate speed."

"Jim, are there other allegations?"

"There is an allegation concerning you helping your sister avoid jury duty."

"Again, that's nonsense. My sister lived in the Palmer area and was called to report all the way out in Springfield. I just inquired about helping her move to a closer courthouse. We found out that the nearer courthouse didn't need jury duty. She had to report to Springfield, which ultimately she did. I didn't try to get her out of jury duty. That's nonsense."

"Jim, there must be something more to this complaint by Jamie. None of this is true. She must be sick or something."

"John, I'm trying to empathize with you. Please understand this is not the type of call I want to make at six o'clock on a Friday night."

"Is there anything else?"

"There is an allegation that you require your aide to do campaign work."

"That's unbelievable! Regularly she asks how she can help with my campaign work. She says, Is there anything I can do to help? I would never force her to do campaign work."

Fresolo asked Kennedy," Will I be able to be in the room when you interview Jamie?"

"No, that won't be possible. There are other allegations, John."

Kennedy described the allegation made by Ryan that Fresolo has her pressure people when she calls to help people find jobs.

"Jim, you know as well as anyone, that Reps handle inquiries about jobs all the time. I represent an urban district, and my office functions as an employment agency. Jamie helps me with constituents looking for referrals. We make calls and we follow-up on those calls."

Fresolo told Kennedy he was aware of the new ethics directives on referrals, and he was not sure how he would navigate that yet.

"If pressuring employers to hire people is illegal, then like all politicians, I'm guilty of that. We make calls, and we follow-up. We ask employers to give these people interviews. We feel we owe our constituents that. Jamie made those calls and has not complained to me about it."

Fresolo continued, "We have always done that. Now, if the new advisory has changed that, we will adjust our practices accordingly."

"I don't mean this in a bad way, but Jamie must be a psycho."

Fresolo asked if there were other allegations?

Kennedy relayed the allegation about personal services and his daughter's college application.

"Jamie offered to help my daughter fill out her application form because she had never filled one out before. This is a nightmare; she offered to help and now makes it a complaint to the ethics committee?"

"John, you need to have confidence in our office to conduct the investigation."

"Jim, you should talk to someone in the building, I'll get his name for you, he knows that I'm not computer literate. He can vouch that I don't know the technology and that Jamie does all of that."

"John, I have no reason to disbelieve what you are saying."

"I just try to do my best to help people, and it's only my word against hers. She must have some kind of agenda."

"I have no idea if there is any kind of agenda here. We will try to set up a meeting next week, likely Monday or Tuesday to discuss this further. I want to remind you not to have any contact with her from this point forward, no phone calls, no emails, no text messages – nothing. This is for your protection."

"As it is, I sent a text message today, about five o'clock regarding a constituent matter. I was surprised I hadn't heard back from her yet."

"John, you should not expect to hear back from her, and you should use your district aide in the meantime. Jamie will not be in the office next week, and you and she will meet with the Office of Legal Counsel on separate days, so you will not have to see each other."

"I should point out that in the last week or so, I have told Jamie that I did not like the way she was keeping track of constituent matters. I left her a voicemail on her State House phone explaining that I had asked for a list of constituent matters many times before and that I was not going to ask again."

Fresolo continued, "I needed a list of constituent cases that are still ongoing because I have become concerned that things were slipping through the cracks. My tone was not angry or inappropriate."

"The next day, Jamie came in but did not bring the list I asked for. Instead, she gave me all the files that she had made up for each matter. I said it's not what I asked for, but okay, that was fine."

Fresolo speculated whether Ryan brought the complaints because he had criticized the way she was keeping records. He stated that he could not understand why she would come forward with a complaint.

"I'm very respectful of her. I ask everything in the form of a question, not an order. I just recently went to her wedding. I had a fundraiser the next day after her wedding, and I had told her that I might not be able to make it to her wedding, at which point, she started to well-up and looked like she was going to cry."

Fresolo continued, "I drove all the way down to Newport for her wedding, stayed for an hour and then came straight home because I did not want her to think I did not care enough to go to her wedding."

"I've never treated anyone better than I have treated Jamie."

Fresolo asked, "Can she bring her complaints anywhere else?"

"Rather than go down various roads of speculation, let's focus on the investigation at hand," said Kennedy.

"You know, she's never told me that she felt uncomfortable making any of the calls I asked her to make. If she had, I would have said fine, I'll make the call, and would have done it myself."

"John, I know this is a difficult call to receive, and I'll be getting back in touch to schedule a meeting next week."

"I understand. I'll make myself available, and the sooner this all gets resolved, the better."

The John Fresolo Saga

Saturday, March 9, 2012

Early Saturday morning, Fresolo awoke and realized it was not a nightmare that was disturbing his sleep. This was real. For some reason that made no sense, he was being accused by his aide of all kinds of unethical behavior; in fact, seven allegations had been brought to the Office of Legal Counsel, and they were launching a full investigation. Was it too early to call someone?

Fresolo's workout at the gym was especially vigorous this morning as he tried to organize his thinking and develop some counterattack plans to deal with the assault he faced from his aide and the attorneys in the Office of Legal Counsel. He thought to himself, "I'm going to need a lawyer, but who?"

Fresolo decided to make some phone calls to see what help he could get in defending himself from this attack. He wrote a short list. He would call Franny Ford, Billy Breault, Ray McGrath, his cousin Sheila, and maybe that's all for now.

Throughout the day, he spoke with these close friends to express the pain he was feeling and the hollowness in his chest as he tried to understand why Ryan was doing all of this?

When they asked what all the allegations were, he couldn't even remember them. The picture, his other aide, jury duty, and some other things? He had to calm down and think about what the allegations were. He had nothing in writing. Kennedy had simply rattled them off on the phone but sent no text, or email, or anything.

Fresolo thought to himself, what am I supposed to say to my daughters? Should I tell them now? Should I wait? What if this gets out before I speak to them? One of the allegations was that one of them got help with a college application. He hoped they wouldn't have to become involved in this in a public way.

Fresolo spent a good part of the day, exploring how he could get help with how to respond to the allegations. Several attorneys were suggested, all local, but finally Franny Ford, a longtime supporter, attorney, and former clerk of courts, suggested that he contact Attorney Thomas Kiley in Boston. Kiley had a reputation for handling difficult negotiations and top-level clients, especially of a political nature. This was certainly a political issue for Fresolo, and he wanted the best chance to divert this investigation before it got started.

Fresolo was convinced that if the photo he had taken ended up on the State House computer system, Ryan must have plucked it from somewhere and put it on the system. He was convinced he hadn't done it, and also knew he was incapable of doing it. He didn't know how to use Facebook or any of the other systems that were becoming popular. He had enough trouble with his phone. In fact, the phone was the only thing he used to communicate with people. He would text messages and text photos. How it got from his phone to the State House computer had to have been deliberate by Ryan. He had to get to the bottom of this. He needed solid legal advice.

Monday, March 11, 2013

Everything about going into Boston on Monday morning was unlike any morning he had experienced for the past 15 years. He was up early, which was his usual practice, but he was not coordinating a ride with someone as he usually did for the past 15 years. His normal behavior was to ride in with another Legislator as part of a ride-sharing that had been common practice for decades. Until his falling out with John Binienda, as a result of the Speaker fight, the two of them had swapped back and forth on which car to take in. They frequently had other passengers who they would pick up along the way as well.

Alone, he had to drive into Boston trying to imagine how he was going to function once he got there. He had no aide to hold down the office routine of incoming voice mails, emails, and notifications. There would be no one to focus his attention on calendar items, meetings to attend, events to appear at, committee activities, and various hearings.

Instead, he was facing a giant void where all of his energies must focus on how and why his aide had dumped seven allegations on the Office of Legal Counsel, which now was committed to investigating him. How could this be? Why would Ryan want to sabotage him in this way?

John thought of making more phone calls, but held off and decided to get into Boston as early as possible and make calls from there. The first order of business was to get Thomas Kiley on the phone to see if he would be willing to help John out of this crisis.

Richard F. Wright

Chapter Three

Legal Counsel - Interviews

Monday, March 11, 2013, to March 15, 2013

Monday, March 11, 2013, was a busy day for the Office of Legal Counsel. Jim Kennedy thought he had passed the knot in his stomach on to Representative Fresolo, but he still had his.

Attorneys Kennedy and Fleming spent the day preparing to launch the investigation ordered by Speaker DeLeo into the allegations raised by Representative Fresolo's administrative aide, Ryan. They planned to contact and schedule interviews with anyone that might have something to contribute to the investigation and if possible, get all the interviews done before the end of the week. With about a dozen witnesses and maybe more, it was going to be a tight timeframe and even tighter scheduling challenge.

Before they had gotten too far along in setting up their investigation process, they were interrupted by Laura Richter, a Legislative Aide. She made an unannounced visit to the

Office of Legal Counsel and reported that Representative Fresolo was trying to gain access to Ryan's voicemail messages. Richter stated that she came into the office to find all of Ryan's "stuff was gone," and that the receptionist in that area was asking her how to get into Ryan's voicemail.

The receptionist, Rachel Scott, told Richter that Fresolo had called to ask how to access Ryan's voicemail. Richter continued by telling Kennedy that she and Scott felt it was "weird," and before proceeding further, they wanted to talk to someone in the Office of Legal Counsel to make sure it was okay.

Kennedy assured them that she did the right thing and had nothing to be concerned about. He advised her that this had nothing to do with her and that he would follow up with the Representative to get him what he needs. He offered no further clarifying information for Richter.

Kennedy spoke to Bob England in the LIS (Legislative Information Services Department) and confirmed Fresolo had not tried to gain access to any of Ryan's electronic files and that he had only requested access to constituent-related voicemail messages on the office phone.

Kennedy and Fleming spent most of Monday charting a plan to conduct interviews and to gather specific information that would be useful in uncovering facts that would sustain or dismiss the allegations that Ryan had brought forth. They had to do the calling and scheduling themselves to minimize the number of people involved in the investigation at this stage.

The first interviews were set for the next day, Tuesday, March 12, 2013, to be held in the Office of Legal Counsel.

Other appointments were set for Wednesday and Friday. More may have to be scheduled as needed.

Tuesday, March 12, 2013

Kennedy held the first interview of the investigation on the phone with former Associate Counsel of the Office of Legal Counsel, Paul Iannuccillo. Kennedy wanted to confirm whether Iannuccillo had met with Ryan the past November and what the conversation had revealed to him.

"Paul, did you have a visit from Representative Fresolo's aide, Jamie Ryan, last November (2012)?

"Yes, I did meet with her. She came to my office."

"What did she want to know from you?"

"She posed a hypothetical case of what happens when an employee had an issue with her boss. She asked, what happens if an employee doesn't like the way she's being treated? What should that person do about it?"

Iannuccillo explained that when he spoke to Ryan about it, he told her that a hypothetical is one thing but "anything you tell me I have to report to my supervisors."

"I told her about Dana Fleming in our office and that she could talk to her. I said if you have an issue, let me know, and you can talk to Dana."

He went on to describe to Kennedy that Ryan never came in again to give him more specifics about her questions. He explained that "she never said I'm being treated this way."

She did not make clear that the hypothetical was about herself.

Kennedy wanted to understand about the hypothetical she posed.

"Paul, can you remember any of the hypotheticals she posed?"

"She gave me a hypothetical, like, how a boss is treating an employee, and wanted to know, 'if she complained about it,' could she be retaliated against?"

Kennedy pressed Paul if he thought the hypotheticals were about her?

"My gut feeling was that it was her."

Iannuccillo explained, "I pressed her on it, but she wouldn't tell me. I said to her, if it's really going on, you should tell me, but she said no, this is just a hypothetical."

He told Kennedy that the hypothetical had something to do with the fact that the hypothetical person was called on his or her cell phone repeatedly. Kennedy did not ask further about that question.

Kennedy asked how long the meeting with Ryan was? Iannuccillo said, "the meeting was five or ten minutes. It was just one time that I remember."

Kennedy wanted to know how Iannuccillo knew Ryan and how she came to ask for a meeting with him?

"Oh, I've known her for four or five years. I used to do some work with her when she worked in the legislative office she worked in before she started working for Representative Fresolo. I don't think she's making stuff up."

"Paul, would you say you consider Ryan trustworthy?"

"I would say I'm 80 to 85 percent confident that she was telling the truth. The only thing that gives me pause is that I'm not sure how she parted ways with Representative Murphy, the Rep she previously worked for, because Jamie told me that she had decided not to invite Murphy to her wedding."

"Paul, what if any relationship do you have with Representative Fresolo."

Paul said, "None."

Kennedy asked Iannuccillo whether he had further contact with Ryan after that meeting. He explained that he didn't have much contact. He stated that he might have said hello or goodbye to her in the hallway, but that was it.

"I did once tell her that she would need to share her comments, that is, move them up the ladder, and she reacted that she did not want to talk anymore. It appeared to me that Jamie was concerned that if she did do something, she would be retaliated against or fired."

At this point in the conversation, Fleming spoke up. She asked Iannuccillo if Ryan mentioned anything about emails or photographs in any of her hypotheticals?

"No, we didn't get into anything like that. We didn't go that far or get into any of that stuff."

Kennedy thanked Iannuccillo for his time on the phone and reminded him of the importance to keep the discussion confidential. Iannuccillo said he understood.

The next day, Wednesday, March 13, 2013, Iannuccillo telephoned Fleming in the Legal Counsel office because he had remembered an additional hypothetical that Ryan had shared with him. Fleming came to the phone.

Iannuccillo told Fleming that Ryan had asked, "What happens if the hypothetical employee applies for a new job in the building (the State House), would this hypothetical person's boss become upset?"

Paul said, "Well if this hypothetical person wanted to find out about any openings, he or she could always go to HR (Human Resources)."

Paul went on to explain that the conversation with Ryan had taken place before new House members were being sworn in, and he described to her that there may be new openings when the new people come on. She then asked Iannuccillo if there would be a "record," of her going to HR," Paul stated that he didn't know.

Tuesday, March 12, 2013

On Tuesday, March 12, in the late morning, Patty DePamphilis made her way over to the Legal Counsel office without knowing why she was being called to a meeting with the attorneys who work there. She knew who they were and what they do in that office because as the Speaker's Chief of Staff's administrative assistant, she often has reason to interact with the Legal Counsel office.

"Why am I being summoned to the Legal Counsel office," asked DePamphilis as soon as she came into the room.

Kennedy said, "The Speaker has ordered me to investigate an important matter that concerns one of the Representatives and his aide. As part of the investigation, we need to ask you a few questions, and I want to point out that this is a confidential matter, so it's important that you keep this conversation confidential."

DePamphilis knew from his tone that Kennedy wanted her to accept that he was doing what he had to do and that he wanted her to cooperate.

Kennedy said, "I need to ask you some questions about Jamie Ryan, Representative Fresolo's aide."

"I don't want to get anyone into trouble," said DePamphilis. "I hope that Jamie is alright, and I just want to say that you are making me nervous."

Kennedy and Fleming spoke up to assure DePamphilis that there was nothing to be nervous about, that Jamie was fine, and not in any trouble at all. Speaking calmly, they both told DePamphilis that this was a personnel issue and out of respect to Jamie, it was "important that the discussion not go beyond the room."

Somewhat assured by the comments from both attorneys, DePamphilis said she understood better now and proceeded to describe her relationship with Ryan.

"I've known Jamie for a long time. I've known her since Ways and Means (Committee). She worked for Rep Murphy. We just started talking one day because she was in Ways and Means a lot. She seemed like a nice kid, to me."

She explained that she knew Ryan had stopped working for Representative Murphy at some point and that she had then come back to take a position in the State House with Representative Fresolo.

It was during the time that she worked for Representative Murphy that Ryan had gotten engaged and they occasionally talked about that and her plans for a wedding. "It was all just friendly girl conversation," said DePamphilis. She also mentioned that she had sent a card to Ryan when her father had died. Kennedy asked when that was, but Patty could not remember.

DePamphilis then stated that about four or five months ago, Ryan asked her if she wanted to go out for a coffee. She agreed and set a day and time. When they met, they spent most of the time looking at Ryan's wedding pictures.

DePamphilis said, "Then toward the end of our time, Jamie asked me about other opportunities in the building (State House)."

Ryan said, "You know, Patty, Rep Fresolo is not one of Speaker DeLeo's favorite guys. I want a chance to do more than just constituent services."

DePamphilis stated that she just tried to give Ryan some motherly advice and recommended that she keep her eyes open for postings in the building and that she send "a letter to Toby, (Deputy Chief of Staff, Toby Morelli), or the Speaker," asking about other opportunities in the building. She also pointed out not to overlook the municipalities because they sometimes have good openings.

Kennedy said, "Do you know why Jamie decided to leave Representative Murphy's office?

"I have no idea," said Patty.

"When you met with Jamie, did she make any allegations against Representative Fresolo?"

"Absolutely not. She just wanted more. She knew it was unlikely that Fresolo would get a chairmanship and she was eager for other opportunities.

"Have you seen or spoken to Jamie since you had the coffee meeting?"

"I saw her just the other day. I had seen the posting come out for the women's caucus and saw her in the hall. I asked if she was considering that and Jamie was non-committal."

"Did Jamie email you about the posted women's caucus position?"

DePamphilis said, "No, there were no emails or anything like that, it was just a random conversation in the hallway."

Kennedy asked DePamphilis, "Have you ever had an occasion to discuss Jamie Ryan with Toby?"

"Yes, I did talk to Toby about Jamie once. There was a position, and I asked how about Jamie Ryan?"

Kennedy asked, "What happened."

"I recollect that Toby said something like, I don't know." When asked, DePamphilis could not recall the type of position and when it had come open.

"You know, it's not unusual for people to ask me about opportunities in the building. It happens all the time. It's common. I would estimate 20 people approached me about job opportunities in the past year," said DePamphilis.

Kennedy sought to better understand the nature and situation of Ryan coming to DePamphilis for advice on other opportunities.

"Was there anything about Jamie's inquiries that stood out by comparison to others who have approached you?"

"No, it was ordinary, and I had no concerns about it," said DePamphilis.

Kennedy turned to another subject with DePamphilis. He wanted to know what she knew about Fresolo's district aide.

"Do you know Representative Fresolo's district aide?"

"I didn't know that he had one." She joked that she doesn't go outside of Boston that much.

"Getting back to Jamie, my conversation with her was very straightforward. She wanted to know if I knew about other positions. We explored her options together; it was no different than a conversation I would have with my son or daughter."

DePamphilis continued, "I don't know what her network is like in the building or how many people she knows. Jamie is a hard worker and tends bar at Marina Bay. I think she's a nice kid. I talk to everybody. She knew Fresolo would not make Chair. She was eager to move on. That was it."

As the interview was drawing to a close, DePamphilis spoke up.

"I'm worried about Jamie."

Kennedy and Fleming both assured her that Ryan had done nothing wrong and was perfectly fine.

Tuesday, March 12, 2013

On Tuesday, March 12, Keith Johnson, Director of Human Resources at the State House met with Kennedy and Fleming of the Legal Counsel office. Kennedy informed Johnson that the House was dealing with an employment issue in Representative Fresolo's office.

"Keith, do you have any recollection of Jamie Ryan stopping by to ask for a transfer out of Representative Fresolo's office?"

Johnson responded that Fleming had stopped by the HR office the day before and brought this question up about Ryan. "So, I looked back over my pads of paper but did not have any notes of a conversation with Jamie."

"It's possible she could have stopped by; people sometimes just do that. But it was certainly nothing more formal than that because if it had been, I would have had notes," said Johnson.

Kennedy asked directly, "Do you recall ever speaking with Jamie Ryan about her job in Representative Fresolo's office?"

"I don't have any recollection of a meeting or of speaking to her about a new position.

Fleming spoke up, "How well do you know Jamie?"

"I know her well enough to say hi, how are you, but not much beyond that."

Kennedy said, "Well then I suppose that if you don't remember speaking or meeting with Jamie about her desire for a new position, you wouldn't, therefore, remember taking any actions on her behalf, is that correct?"

"That's correct. I don't recall taking any actions.

Kennedy asked, "Do people routinely come to the HR office to ask for new positions?"

Johnson said, "People tend to come in when there is a leadership change, and people will occasionally pop in. It doesn't happen all that often, usually around the time of a leadership change."

Kennedy asked, "Keith, do you have an opinion as to Jamie's trustworthiness?"

"I don't know her well enough to judge her credibility."

"Do you know why Jamie left Representative Murphy's office?"

"I believe that she left to make more money at some other job in the private sector. I also remember that she returned to the State House in Representative Fresolo's office after only a month. It was a very short time-span."

Kennedy probed further about Ryan's departure from Murphy's office. "Is there anyone else in the HR office that might know why Jamie left Murphy's office? Is it possible that she said something to someone else in the office?"

"It's possible, but I don't recall anyone ever relaying that information to me so I would say it's generally unlikely. I recall the time of her leaving, and I don't remember there being any bad terms. I believe she left voluntarily."

Kennedy asked if Johnson was aware of any complaints, Ryan might have made, and Johnson said he was not aware of any complaints. Kennedy asked if Johnson was aware of any performance issues that Ryan had experienced either in Representative Murphy or Representative Fresolo's office.

Johnson said, "Neither of the Reps had ever called me about Jamie's performance."

He did recall that while Ryan was working for Representative Murphy that there was another aide, Mary Roy, who once complained about Ryan's tardiness. Johnson stated that Mary Roy stopped him in the hallway and said something about tardiness in passing.

"At the time, I advised Mary that she should speak to Jamie about the importance of being on time."

Johnson could not recall when the conversation took place, but he was confident that it was the only performance issue he could recall regarding Ryan and that he had not spoken to Mary Roy about it again.

Kennedy switched topics from Ryan to Fresolo's other aide, Kenneth Simoncini. Kennedy asked Johnson if he knew Fresolo's district aide?

Johnson said, "I do not know him, and I can't even say if I've ever seen him. I recall no contact with him whatsoever."

Kennedy brought up the general HR office policy, which requires staff who work in the building to sign in. Kennedy asked, "How are we ensuring that staff who work in the district offices sign in?"

Johnson said, "Most district staffers do sign in, but occasionally, people who are promoted from the Legislative Aide position to a new position, forget to fill out timesheets because as Legislative Aides they are not required to do so. Johnson explained that Ken Simoncini was someone who started out as a Legislative Aide."

Johnson stated that he would have "had a conversation" with the Speaker's Office and/or Representative Fresolo about the fact that Ken needed to start filling out timesheets when he became an administrative aide, but that he could not recall the specific conversation.

"Do you have any timesheets for Ken Simoncini?"

"No, I do not."

Johnson added, "Ken is apparently someone who doesn't sign in and out. He's an administrative aide, and he should be doing that."

"The timesheet requirement is something that I would have informed the employee or the Rep about that. It would have been a verbal conversation and that it probably happened over the phone."

Kennedy asked about Simoncini's personnel file. Johnson reviewed the file for him pointing out that Simoncini made the switch from Legislative Aide to District Aide on June 20, 2006, about seven years prior.

"I would have informed him of the timesheet requirement at the time," said Johnson.

Johnson continued, "I would have reached out to the Representative. It would have been a phone call."

Johnson further stated that "the Rep may have responded that he didn't want Ken to fill out a timesheet."

Kennedy continued to listen as Johnson reviewed the personnel file.

Johnson said, "If that happened, I would have gone to the Speaker's office, what, if anything happened after that, I could not say."

Kennedy asked, "Who in the Speaker's office would you have spoken to about the Rep suggesting Ken did not have to fill out a timesheet?"

"I would have spoken to Mary Anne Calia or Danny Toscano in the Speaker's office[3], it would have been something that I would have gone to them about."

---

[3] Salvatore DiMasi was the Speaker at the time

Fleming interjected a question at this point in the review of the Simoncini personnel file. "Are there other district aides who should be filling out timesheets, but are currently not?"

"There are none that I am aware of, but I will double-check that."

Furthering the question about timesheets, Kennedy asked, "Can you think of any other district aides in the past who did not fill out timesheets?"

Johnson answered, "There were a few women who worked for a former Rep who had something other than Legislative Aide as their title, but who still did not fill out timesheets.

"At the time I talked to them and the Rep about the need for all employees, except Legislative Aides, to fill out timesheets."

Johnson continued, "The Rep said that he didn't want these employees to have to sign in and out. I advised the Rep and the employees that if there is no record of their working hours, then the House would not be able to enter vacation or sick time for them."

Kennedy directed Johnson to confirm whether any other district employees should be filling out timesheets, but who, for whatever reason, are not doing so. Johnson explained that while he is not aware of anyone other than Simoncini, he would check his records.

Kennedy and Fleming discussed what capability the HR office had to sort employees, by office location, (State House vs. District), and Johnson determined they could not do such a sort.

Johnson said, "District Aides are not segregated on a separate list. A search of the list would take quite some time."

Johnson continued, "I think the number of district office employees who were failing to complete timesheets would be small if any, and that the other situations like that arose when a staffer went from being a Legislative Aide to another position."

Kennedy said, "I want you to start with the district office staffers who had failed to sign-in in the last month and work backward from there."

Johnson agreed he would.

Fleming turned the interview to a different topic. "Are you aware of any complaints that any staffer had ever made against Representative Fresolo?"

"No, there were none."

"What can you tell us about Representative Fresolo's former aide, Annie Martin-McDonough?"

"I know who she is and that she still works in the building for another member of the House. I don't know why she left Representative Fresolo's office."

Fleming asked, "Do you know Martin-McDonough any better than you know Jamie Ryan?"

"I don't know her any better, and I only know her well enough to say, Hi."

Fleming asked, "Do you know Representative Fresolo and have you had any contact with him?"

"No, I haven't had any contact with Representative Fresolo in months."

Kennedy thanked Johnson for coming in, and the meeting concluded.

Tuesday, March 12, 2013

Attorneys Kennedy and Fleming were about to conduct the fourth interview of the day. The interview with Jamie Ryan was held at about 3 o'clock in the afternoon. Fleming had previously interviewed Ryan, but today this was an interview scheduled under the auspices of a preliminary investigation launched by the Speaker of the House to determine if there was just cause to hold a hearing on the associated allegations brought against Representative John Fresolo.

Kennedy started the meeting with an apology.

"The Speaker has asked me to convey his regret that you are in this situation. Along with the Speaker, we all share his sentiments and regret that you have been placed in this situation."

Ryan responded, "Thank you, I appreciate that."

"As you know," said Kennedy," due to the serious nature of the allegations, the Speaker has ordered us to conduct an investigation and that the Office of Legal Counsel is in the process of speaking to several people."

Ryan spoke up, "If I may interrupt, may I ask who else the Office of Legal Counsel has spoken to as part of the investigation?"

"We have prepared a list of witnesses that we plan to interview."

Without answering directly whom they had already spoken to or were planning to speak with, which was Ryan's question, Kennedy continued.

"Obviously, we needed to speak to Representative Fresolo and a few other people who may have information that is tangentially related to the issues you raised."

Continuing, Kennedy said, "For example, we spoke to Rachel Wood the day before. She is the receptionist in the Committee on Bonding. We spoke with her to clarify how incoming constituent calls and messages would be handled in your absence."

Ryan said, "That was good, I'm glad you spoke to Rachel. I have just received a couple of emails from an interest group, and I wonder what you want me to do with them?"

"For now, we want you to put an - out of office - message on and to direct all incoming inquiries directly to the Representative."

Kennedy offered the following suggestion: "I am currently out of the office, please send your email and any other information directly to Representative Fresolo at (list his email address)."

"This will take care of incoming mail, and besides, we don't want to disable your email as you will be back in a new position soon," said Kennedy.

Ryan said, "I have a memo here that shows the outstanding matters that I can think of, but my files are in the Representative's office so I can't be certain I got everything."

Kennedy and Fleming discussed the memo and its contents with Ryan, and then they turned to the interview.

Kennedy said, "I'm going to ask you a series of questions, and although some of those questions may have already been discussed with Dana Fleming, I want you to please bear with me. If I ask you a question a second time, please do not read anything into that. I may ask a second time, not because I don't believe your prior statements, but just because I want to make sure I have the chronology right."

Ryan said, "Thank you for explaining it the way you did. I feel more confident about this whole process now. I'm feeling better. This seems to be an official process. In the old days, this might have been handled differently."

"The Speaker is aware of the concerns you have raised, and he has ordered me to conduct an investigation with all deliberate speed and that it's taken very seriously," said Kennedy.

Kennedy and Fleming settled down to asking questions starting with a review of Ryan's professional employment history. Ryan explained that she started working for a law firm right out of college for about a year and then went to work for Rockland Trust bank. After that, she found out about an opening at the State House through a friend, which she thought would be a good fit. She took the aide position and worked for that Rep for three and a half years.

At this point in the conversation, Kennedy paused to let Ryan know that if she needed a break at any time, she should let them know. He also wanted to remind Ryan that he and Fleming were both Counsels for the House and that they serve as counsel to the institution, not to the individual staffers.

"I want to be clear that we are not here as your personal attorneys and, in fact, could not serve as your personal attorney."

"Let me then ask, do I need a lawyer?"

Kennedy informed Ryan of her rights. "I can't answer that question, but if you want to have a lawyer, you have that right."

Ryan said, "I knew I had that right, and like the Miranda warning, a person always has that right."

Fleming spoke up, saying, "If at any point you feel uncomfortable and want to speak to a lawyer, we can stop. This will be true today and throughout the investigation process."

Ryan laughed, directing a comment toward Kennedy, "Dana knows that I'm a crier."

Fleming and Kennedy further reiterated that they represent the House. Both said, "You are welcome to get legal counsel."

Fleming asked, "Do you want to stop and get counsel, or are you comfortable moving forward?

"I'm comfortable moving forward without an attorney present."

"Fine, then let's continue," said Kennedy.

Kennedy asked for Ryan to confirm that she left her previous legislative employer in January 2011, two years prior. Ryan agreed.

"Did you experience any issues with your previous legislative employer?"

"No, I didn't. I left because I wanted a change, a chance to do something different. I took a job in the private sector, doing some work with medical records. That job is not on my resume as I was only there for six weeks."

Ryan explained that the job meant more money, but it was not very interesting. She stated that she wasn't really happy with the new job.

Ryan said, "I was only there a few weeks. I belong in the State House."

Kennedy asked Ryan to confirm when she started working for John Fresolo. Ryan said that the Rep had called her in February 2011. He offered her the job, and she decided to take it. She pointed out that Fresolo had offered her the job as his aide before her leaving for the private sector job. She had accepted it, but then he notified her the next day that he had to withdraw it as he didn't realize that the Legislator she was working for was not leaving his office. He didn't want to, in effect, be taking someone's aide away from them. Now that she was out of the building, he could offer her a job to come back.

Kennedy asked, "Was your previous legislative employer upset that you were leaving?"

"No, there were no issues. I was just looking for a change."

Kennedy turned the questions toward how the working conditions were in Representative Fresolo's office. He asked when she first started to have some concerns about Representative Fresolo?

"I don't really know when it started," said Ryan. "But, I never said no to a lot of his requests. I was nervous. He was my boss, and I'm the only office aide," she added.

Ryan described she probably started having concerns within the first few months but that she went along with it out of concern for her job security.

Kennedy asked if she had any specific examples?

Ryan stated that she couldn't recall anything specific that first triggered her concerns but noted that the Rep asked her to do a lot of things that she was not asked to do by her prior legislative employer.

"For example, he asked me to draft a lot more letters of recommendation."

Ryan continued, "I don't remember the exact date or incident when I first became concerned, but it might have been when the Rep asked me to design his campaign invitation. He had a fundraiser in May 2011, the first year I started working for him. I had to work with the printer, then pick up the invitations and then stuff them."

Kennedy asked Ryan if she had expressed her concerns to anyone?

"No, I did not. I was concerned about my job, whether I would lose my job."

Ryan began to describe that she has a second job. She said she worked at *Port 305* in Marina Bay in Quincy.

"I worked for them every summer. Even now, on Fridays, Saturdays, and Sundays, I work there. My husband is an electrician, and he and I are trying to save for a house."

Kennedy turned to another subject. He wanted to know who handled the technology in the office?

Ryan asked, "Do you mean the Rep's Facebook and his website?"

"Yes, you can start by discussing that, but what I'm looking for from you is also looking at the general picture of what, if any, computer issues you handle in the office?"

"Well, I'm generally in charge of all the computer issues for the office. I set up and designed the website."

Ryan went on, "The Rep's website is an everything website."

Kennedy asked, "What do you mean by it's an everything website?"

"The website is a private or personal website, and it is not run through the State House system or on any of the State House servers. I updated and redesigned the site."

"Was the representative or anyone else involved in setting up the site?"

"No, nobody else was involved in the setup, just me."

"Did you set up the Representative's Facebook page?"

"The Rep already had a Facebook page when I came to work for him. He would have me upload photos and update his status."

"Did you have access to the Representative's email?"

"I had access to write emails on his behalf. I can send the emails from his desk or mine."

Ryan continued, "I have the Reps computer login and password, and I'm the one who updates it when the security settings expire."

Ryan continued, "I check the Rep's emails from his workstation or from mine. Sometimes the Rep prefers that an email not come from me, so he asks that I use a different tone, and have it look like it came directly from him."

Kennedy wanted to understand the use of emails and the frequency of use by Ryan and Representative Fresolo.

"How often did you write emails for the Representative?"

"I wrote emails daily, ten times a day, or more."

"Would you say the Representative was tech-savvy?"

"I don't know if the Rep is tech-savvy or not. He got pretty good with his Android phone, but before me working for him in 2011, he had never had a smartphone. I told him then that he should get a Blackberry because I thought it would make the office more efficient."

Ryan described how she helped the Representative purchase a Blackberry within two months of starting to work for him. She explained that the phone crashed and that the Representative got an Android toward the end of 2012.

"It turned out to be hard for the Rep to make the transition from the Blackberry to the Android because the touch-screen feature was new. I was able to help buy the Blackberry and set it up because I had access to his Verizon account. I had account authority."

At this point, Fleming spoke up to ask about Ryan's access to the phone account.

"To what extent did you have access and authority to use the Representative's phone account?"

Kennedy interjected that many Representatives set up corporate-style accounts so their staffers can access the account as needed. Ryan pointed out that she didn't know who paid for the account.

"All I remember is that I ordered the Android for the Rep, and he had me set it up for him. One day he walked in out of the blue with the Android. I brought the phone down to Ben in LIS to set up his email. Ben had the Rep's username and domain to set up the email. Ben set it up, the same way he does for a lot of people."

Ryan pointed out that the Representative's Android "crapped out," and he got a new one to replace it.

Kennedy next turned to questions about the Facebook account.

"Did the Representative specifically instruct you to access Facebook?"

"Yes, he asked me to upload things to Facebook."

Ryan said the Representative would send a text and state: "here upload this."

"I recently uploaded one with Marsha Fowler on his Facebook page and on his website. I would do that from my workstation here in the State House or sometimes from home. I would occasionally ask the Rep if I could do the updates at home because the Internet connection was faster there."

Ryan stated that she would also sometimes go down to LIS, and they would let her use a newer machine.

Kennedy asked, "Does the Representative post anything directly to his Facebook page?"

"I'm not sure if he posts to the Facebook page. I monitor the Facebook page, but not all the time."

"Did you ever see chats or messages?"

"Do you mean Facebook messages?"

"Yes, did you see anything that the Representative posted directly?"

"Yes, I did see Facebook messages. When I have Facebook open, messages appear at the bottom of the page."

At this point in the interview, Kennedy handed a copy of the screenshot images of Facebook messages that Ryan had provided to the Office of Legal Counsel on Friday, March 8, 2013.

Kennedy asked, "Where did you see these messages?"

"They were at the bottom of the page. I opened it up on Friday on his work computer. He was here on Wednesday. I wasn't in on Thursday. When I came in on Friday, I logged on, and that's what was there."

"Can you explain how or why the Representative's Facebook page appeared on the screen when you logged on?"

"I assume that the Rep had locked or left his computer without closing out of Facebook on Wednesday when he was in the building."

"Do you think the Representative had control-alt-delete locked the computer without closing out of the program?"

"That's probably what happened, but I couldn't be sure. All I know for certain is that when I came in on Friday and logged on those messages were there."

"Jamie, let me ask you this, did you type those messages?"

"Oh no, I didn't."

"Do you think the three separate instant message conversations displayed at the bottom of the screen had happened simultaneously?"

"Yes, they probably did."

"Have you ever seen any other inappropriate messages on the Representative's Facebook page other than the ones you have shown us?"

"Yes, I have seen other messages. I didn't go looking for other things, but I have seen other flirtatious messages."

Fleming spoke up and asked if Ryan had seen explicit messages anywhere else?

"No, I have not. I have only seen them on the Facebook page."

Continuing, Fleming asked, "Does the Representative have a private email account, and if so, do you have access to it?"

"Yes, the Rep has a private email account, it's a Yahoo account. I have used it in the past for his campaign emails and campaign invitations."

Ryan continued, "I have sent campaign materials from my State House email address to the Rep's Yahoo account from the State House. I didn't send the campaign materials from the Rep's House email account."

Ryan acknowledged that the Facebook page she provided was from a download she made last week on Friday. She added that the Rep "uses Facebook as a dating website," and then he has me update it. "I thought this was a little strange, but whatever."

Ryan proceeded to describe how the Facebook page came into existence. She stated that the Rep's former aide, Paul McClory, had set up the Facebook page. But she believed it was also possible that the aide who came after Paul had set it up. Her name was Annie Martin-McDonough.

"It's unlikely that Annie would have set up the page because she only worked for the Rep for about six weeks. Annie had to say no to the Rep for some things, and that hadn't gone well for her. Annie went to work for another member of the House."

Ryan further speculated that it was Paul, not Martin-McDonough, who set up the Facebook page, but it could have even been aides before Paul.

"I only logged into Facebook whenever the Rep asked me to. I rarely logged in on my own, I didn't want to go in there."

Fleming followed up with questions about Facebook.

"Jamie, how frequently would you see inappropriate messages?"

"I would sometimes see messages once a week. I saw lots of inappropriate messages that were not as explicit as that. I saw other flirtatious emails and messages."

Fleming asked, "Did you save or print any of those or tell anyone else?"

"I would tell my husband, and I would go home and digest what I had seen."

Kennedy interjected, "Do you think you were meant to see those messages?"

"Definitely not. I don't think he would want anyone to see that. Those are private."

Fleming probed further on the frequency of messages.

"Jamie, could you approximate a percentage of the number of times you went on Facebook how often you would see inappropriate messages?"

"I don't know. But there were enough that I noticed. I just couldn't give a percentage or other estimate."

There was an extended conversation about the mechanics of Facebook. Ryan confirmed for Kennedy and Fleming that to see the messages she would need to be logged into

Facebook through Representative Fresolo's page but would not necessarily need to be using his computer.

Ryan said, "I believe the messages would automatically populate if the Rep hadn't closed them. The reason I logged in from the Rep's station on last Friday (March 8, 2013) was that I wanted to find a digital copy of the photo to send to the Office of Legal Counsel."

Fleming asked, "Did the Representative know that you sometimes logged in from his workstation?"

"Yes, absolutely. I would have to change his password. The only way to change your work password is to physically come in and change it. The Rep had me do that all the time, whenever the security settings expired."

Kennedy moved on to the subject of the photograph that Ryan had found in the Representative's Facebook page.

"Jamie, tell me how you first came upon the photograph, how you first discovered it."

"I got married on November 3, (2012) and when I returned from my honeymoon, the Rep wanted me to resend an email about a piece of legislation that he was filing regarding the Worcester Housing Authority. The bill was supposed to require the Housing Authority to buy American products and goods to promote the local economy so long as the prices weren't ten percent higher."

Ryan continued, "I thought it was actually a good bill and that someone in the Office of Legal Counsel had drafted it for me. I love when the Office of Legal Counsel drafts bills for me because then I looked wicked smart."

Continuing, Ryan said, "I went into the Rep's sent mail to find that bill and send it out looking for co-sponsors. When I saw the photo, I opened it because it's par for the course for me to update Facebook and the website. I figured I would get ahead of it, but obviously, that was not what I found. Eventually, I found the right email regarding the legislation and sent it out."

Kennedy asked, "Did you think the Representative meant to send that picture from his email?"

"I don't think it was intended to go over mass.gov. I don't want to give the Rep more credit than he deserves, but he may have meant to send it as a text message."

"Had you ever seen anything like this before?"

"No, I have not."

"Have you told anyone about this?"

"I told one aide, and I prefer not to tell you the person's name."

"Jamie, you know it's important that we speak with everyone who has information relevant to the investigation and that the person would not be trouble in any way."

"I really prefer not to throw out anyone's name. Would it be alright if I checked with them first because I'd like to give them a heads-up?"

"That would be fine. Remember, no one is in trouble. Whoever it is, is not in any sort of trouble."

"I don't want to see this person get roped in."

"There's nothing to get roped into."

"I don't want any sort of public report or filing from the Office of Legal Counsel. The Rep is a single guy. It's not an excuse, but I don't care what he does, it's just that I don't want to have to see it."

Ryan became concerned about how the matter was going to be handled and whether it had to become public. "Will there be a public report?"

Kennedy responded, "I don't know. If there is a report from my office, I do not expect that it would be available for the public, not any time soon at least."

"I'm the Rep's only staff person. It will be pretty easy to figure out that the complaint came from me."

"Again, I do not expect there to be a public report with your name on it. This is an internal investigation that will generate a confidential internal report. The Speaker will decide where it goes from there."

Kennedy came back to the question of who else Ryan has spoken to about the photograph.

"Can you confirm to me that you only told one person about the photograph and you will get us the name of that person?"

"Yes."

Kennedy then asked Ryan has she ever talked to Representative Fresolo about the messages she encountered on Facebook or the photo she found in his sent box?"

"I wouldn't know how to have that conversation with him: 'Hey, guess what I saw,' and I didn't want to discuss his penis with him. I just kept quiet."

"Can you confirm to me that Representative Fresolo never brought it up to you?"

"No, he never brought it up to me. I don't think the Rep intended to send it using his State House account."

"How often are you on the Representative's email account?"

"I log onto his email account daily."

"Okay Jamie, I want to ask you some questions about Ken Simoncini, the Representative's district aide. Have you ever met him?"

"Actually, I did meet him once at a fundraiser in May. When I first talked to Dana (Fleming), I thought I had not met him, but after thinking about it further, I realized I had met him once at this fundraiser. Although, even though I met him at that time, if you did a line-up, I wouldn't know him."

"I understand. Aside from the one time you met him in person, how often do you speak to Ken?"

"I rarely speak to Ken. I did speak to him once when Ken's daughter or niece needed help getting out of jury duty. Ken's daughter or niece, whichever, has a son with severe problems, cystic fibrosis or some other disease and she said she couldn't take time off work to serve on a jury."

"Are there any emails or text messages on this subject?"

"I can go through my inbox to see."

"Jamie, was Ken's relative trying to get her jury duty postponed or canceled entirely?"

"She was trying to get out of it entirely. She ended up showing up and being dismissed on the spot. But she was unhappy that she even had to show up at all. The Rep made me forward the information to him. I believe the Rep made the call to the courthouse or jury commissioner. I don't think I made that particular call."

Ryan continued, "I recently tried to contact Ken about a constituent matter involving DOR and taxes, but he never got back to me. I had decided to reach out to him because he's an accountant by trade. I didn't have his phone number, so I Googled it."

"I do recall another time when I spoke to Ken around the holidays when the House was scheduled to have a skeleton crew. I joked with him about which skeleton day he wanted? When I spoke to him, he was away, I believe at Disney."

Ryan went on to comment that Simoncini did come in occasionally for ethics training but that it was hard to get him to come in for it.

"I recall that the Rep had called the Committee on Personnel and Administration around the clock right around then. I know that Ken did not come in with the rest of the staff and that he did the training separately."

"Jamie, do you know why Ken does not have email?"

"I don't know. I had to provide the Office of Legal Counsel with Ken's contact information recently so that they could send him his ethics summary. I was not aware of his phone number, so that's why I Googled it."

"What can you tell me about the Representative's district office?"

"You mean his house? His district office is 25 Dolly Drive, which is the same address as his house."

"Is that where Ken works?"

"No, I don't think so, but Ken's address is right across the street."

"Have you ever spoken to the Representative about Ken?"

"Yes, I have. He told me that Ken is the guy who handles his campaign account. I told him that he should not repeat that statement to other people because I knew that was not correct. The Rep's sister, Sandy, is the campaign treasurer."

"What else do you know about the work Ken does for the Representative?"

"I don't know who Ken is. He might do the OCPF filings, but I'm not sure. I have never heard the Rep talk to anyone else about Ken and Ken and I don't work together on constituent matters. He doesn't call the office regularly or refer any work to me. His W-2 comes to the office."

Ryan continued, "If you call the district office, it is actually the Rep's home phone. The message says, if you need immediate attention, please contact Jamie Ryan. There is no mention of Ken on the message. I don't know what kind of a deal they have."

"Where do Ken's paystubs get delivered?"

"They come to me, and I stick them in a desk drawer. I may have taken some of them with me when I cleared out my things."

"If you have any, please return them to the Office of Legal Counsel tomorrow."

"Okay."

Kennedy turned to other matters beginning with the jury duty allegation.

"What can you tell me about the Representative helping his sister with jury duty?"

"The Rep wanted help to get his sister, Tricia, moved to a new court. I don't recall exactly which courthouse she was assigned to or where she wanted to go to, but I recall that they got her moved to Springfield, but that she didn't want to go there because of all the Puerto Ricans and gangbangers."

"Do you know if the Representative's sister, Tricia, was a constituent?"

"No, she is not a constituent. The Rep's sister wanted Palmer, but they don't have jury trials there. I called the trial court, the jury commissioner, they instructed me to have her write a letter to the trial court, write a letter to change her date. She called me that she got a new date for May and she still wanted out of jury duty. I told her I would pass that on to the Rep."

At this point in the interview, Ryan pulled out a notebook with some information.

"We got her the location she wanted, but in May she is hoping that the Rep will make a call and get her out of it completely. She lives in Brimfield. The Rep told me to call Henry King in East Brookfield. I think I emailed him about that."

Ryan continued, "The Rep has asked me to do this in the past. Maybe I did call. Typically, it was just getting the information and passing it along. This was the only time I called the jury commissioner. I don't know why; I probably was proactive in trying to figure this out. A lot of it, I just try to figure it out on my own."

Kennedy concluded his questions about jury duty and turned to the issue of job recommendations made by the Representative.

"Jamie, did you have concerns with the way that the Representative was recommending people?"

"I had a personal opinion. It was my opinion that we were not effective. I felt like we were the worst employment agency in the world."

"Did you and the Representative discuss the new advisory on this?"

"Yes, he mentioned it after the caucus. I don't think he went to the caucus. He asked me what we're supposed to be doing now? After having explicit instructions delivered at the caucus I thought we better get on the right page, which is why I called the Office of Legal Counsel.

Ryan explained that she was concerned after seeing the new advisory and memorandum from Jim Kennedy. She was concerned who we can and can't send them to. She was worried about figuring out how to verify that the person was actually qualified for the position. She stated that Fleming had helped her sort through those requirements.

"I felt that some of my work following up the Rep's employment recommendations was unnecessary and seemed counter-productive. He would have me call every two to three days. There was a new hospital in Worcester. He had me emailing the legislative liaison to DMH to find out when their interview would be, how it went, anything else we can do to help? It just seemed like a lot of follow-ups. I just didn't think we were supposed to do all that follow-up. If I was on the hiring end, I might say I was being pressured.

"Did you feel like you were pressuring anyone?"

"No, but we were doing way more follow-up than other Reps. We would recommend five or six people for the same job. It was consuming most of my day. I felt like the most unsuccessful headhunter."

"Did the Representative advise you to change your practices after the advisory?"

"No. He told me to continue as status quo. Send it off, send a copy to the constituent, keep a file copy. Keep following up until we get an answer. Phone calls and emails."

"Did the Representative tell you what to say?"

"No, he just told me to call and check in. UMass doesn't want me emailing any information to them anymore. They only want me to call. UMass has a union, so sometimes it doesn't really matter because they have to give it to a union person. But they said, no more emails."

Kennedy next turned his questions to the issue of performing campaign work.

"What campaign work has the Representative asked you to do?"

"I've done his mailings, all the labeling for his campaign fundraisers, and stuffing the invitation. He would mail me rolls of stamps to get them out. He's had three or four events since I started working there and I worked on all of them. He had one the day after my wedding, but I didn't go. I helped get the mailing out though. So that would have been on November 2, 2013."

Ryan pointed out that the Representative keeps his campaign list on the system.

"It's named Christmas List."

"Jamie, have you ever raised concerns about doing campaign work?

"I just felt like I couldn't say no. I'm sure he would have found someone that would do it. I just put together something for another candidate. I would have done that after-hours because I like that person, but he asked me during work. I just put together an event that would have happened last night. I worked with the candidate's campaign staff on an event that included the candidate's wife speaking at a senior center. I did that from the State House and working from home."

Ryan continued, "He has had me get home addresses and city council information for the candidate. He asked me to post a photo on his Facebook page of him and the candidate. He has me do that."

Continuing, Ryan said, "He just told me that a guy from the campaign would be calling me. I worked with him and then he handed me off to another campaign worker. I had to deal with the Senior Center to schedule it before BINGO. The Rep thinks he is a go-to guy for the candidate in Worcester. He's told me before that he doesn't give me enough work to fill my day, so when he gives me campaign work to do, I feel like I can't say no."

Ryan brings up a new topic concerning Representative Fresolo's previous aide, Annie Martin-McDonough.

"Annie, you know, she worked for the Rep for about six weeks. While this is second-hand, she said to me that the Rep had asked her to lie to a reporter. Apparently, he needed an excuse for why he did not come to a meeting or interview with her. The Rep asked Annie to say that his daughter was in a car accident. She said she wouldn't lie for him."

Ryan explained that when another member offered Annie a job, she took it.

"You know, I didn't feel I was in a position to say no. He was my boss; I work at the pleasure of the Rep."

Ryan then discussed how she helped the Representative's daughter create a job resume.

"I worked on Frankie's resume. I don't know if I made the application, but I definitely worked on Frankie's resume. I created her resume. I used my email to send it to the Rep."

"I also did work for Maria, his other daughter. I worked with Worcester State University to square away her housing and trying to have her transferred to Quinsigamond Community College. I set up a meeting with an admissions director."

Ryan continued, "I did a lot of things to help her, but I didn't physically fill out her college application. I called to get transcripts sent. She only went for a semester at Worcester State."

Kennedy asked Ryan, "Did the Representative say you needed to do a resume for Frankie?"

"Yes, he did. It turned out that the Rep ended up calling all the local colleges to try to find her a job and we are still working with UMass to get her a job at UMass."

Ryan went on to explain, "When Frankie called me she said her Dad said – you're going to be doing this for me. I didn't get any feedback from her or the Rep after I finished the resume. I also just filled out her health insurance forms and added her to GIC (Group Insurance Commission).

Kennedy asked, "Jamie, do you recall telling his daughters that he was a great boss?"

"I say that to everyone. I never want to talk bad about my boss. Number one job is to protect my boss. I definitely said that to his daughters."

Ryan continued, "In terms of time off and vacation he has never denied me. When my wedding came up he was kind about giving me time, he was kind about that. When I first started working for him, people would ask me – how's that – and I would say, it's great, he's great."

"Jamie, have you shared your concerns with anyone else?"

"No, I just did it."

"Was there any reason that you didn't say that you were uncomfortable?"

"He was my boss. I didn't feel confident that I could say no and that he would accept that. There were times when the Rep said if you don't get this done, I will find someone who will."

Ryan added, "There was a time when the Rep – freaked out – that I didn't respond to him for 17 minutes. He was really upset that he couldn't get a hold of me. He wanted to know if I got back to someone about the marijuana bill, but I was across the street getting a salad, and I left my cell phone at my desk to charge. I really wasn't gone that long."

Ryan further explained, "After that, I downloaded a Google Voice free phone number and voicemail, so it transfers calls from my desk. I didn't want him to ever say he couldn't get in touch with me. I tried to be proactive about it. That was November 27. He left me four calls. He was angry."

"Jamie, is there anything else you want to tell us?"

"Yes, there are things about his siblings, his brothers, and sisters. His sister had two speeding tickets. He would have me get information about it. His sister, Sandy, called me and said – I can't believe it, all my years of driving – she wanted to know what to do?"

Ryan explained further, "So, I sent in the appeal form. My advice was to send in the appeal form. That was the standard procedure for other people."

Ryan then discussed the Representative's niece, Amy Skrczk, who works in the Attorney General's office.

"She's out of the Worcester office. She's deserving of the position. The Attorney General called the office. I walked her over for the interview. Amy is a really nice girl. The Rep asked me to write a letter and call on her behalf. He asked me to get him time with the AG's office. This was two years ago for his sister's daughter, Amy."

Ryan described helping the Representative's nephew with a summer job.

"The Rep's nephew wanted a summer job at DOT (Department of Transportation). He had one last summer and wanted one again."

Kennedy asked, "Did you help him get the job at DOT last summer?"

"Yes. At first, they were going to put him in toll collection, but his father, that's the Rep's brother, is a toll collector. So, he ended up getting a maintenance position."

Ryan then described helping the Representative's brother.

"I got the Rep's brother's plumbing business on the NSTAR preferred vendor list. It's Fresolo plumbing. I called a staff person at NSTAR. That staff person called someone who emailed paperwork to Rocky Jr. Maybe that's normal. Rocky was initially denied being put on the list, and there was a waiting list. They just got put on the list after the last big snowstorm."

Ryan then described helping the Representative's Uncle.

"I helped the Rep's Uncle with an application to a private employer. He is kind of disabled. I think I suggested the type of job as a driver. I filled out one of those applications. His name is Richard Fresolo."

Ryan then described helping with per diems.

"About his per diems. In 2011 the Rep said he was here 218 days, but he's here only on full formals. He never goes to hearings. The *Boston Herald* reported 218 days in 2011. Take out 100 days for weekends, and he'd have to be here all the time. He always filled them in. I would submit them to the Treasurer's office mostly by email. Sometimes by fax. He would do them every couple of months. I mean it was a joke, thirty-six dollars to travel to work."

"Did you keep a calendar of when the Rep was in the building?"

"No."

Ryan then described helping with concert tickets.

"I have to get concert tickets from TD Bank North. Different people will call him – can you get me special tickets – to the event. I have to call and get the tickets using his personal credit card. Last time he up-charged it, made an extra sixty dollars. He said I don't really know this guy so charge him extra. The guy called me out on this. The Rep told me to tell him that it was fees."

Ryan continued, "The Rep has a contact at TD Bank North, Joy or Tina. I have called them five or six times for two tickets, four tickets. They mail them to the Rep, and then he gets them to the person. I have to give the credit card information. I have never been denied tickets – yes, we can help out the Representative."

Ryan brought up the Representative's database.

"We had a constituent database where I was tracking all these things, but the Rep said he didn't want me to use the database. He didn't like the reports. He only let me use the one from Dave Tuttle. We had the Barre Group before. It was a really crappy database. The database was my idea. I could send daily reports of updates. Now, he doesn't want to use it. He only allowed me to get the Barre Group, it's a friend of his who owned the company. It was one hundred dollars a month, which was more than the other service cost."

Kennedy had opened up the conversation to Ryan to bring up things she thought they should know about. She focused mostly on the activities on behalf of constituents, relations, and friends of the Representative.

Ryan then continued to add comments.

"On a personal level, my Dad passed away three years ago. The Rep's daughters don't really like their father. So, I tell them he's a good guy. I don't want to talk badly about him, because if I could get one more minute with my Dad, you know?"

Ryan continued, "I just want them to appreciate the time that they have. When I first started working there a lot of people said – how's that – and I said he's great, the best boss I ever had. I wouldn't say that there is dysfunction in our work relationship, that wasn't something I would broadcast to people."

Ryan then asked, "What happens next?"

Kennedy said, "We are going to talk to some more people."

"It's just my word against his, so none of this really matters."

"Jamie, that's not true, it does matter. The Speaker and the Institution take these allegations seriously. The Representative has a right to be heard and to explain these issues. We'll make a determination, and then the Speaker will take that under advisement. Based on that we'll likely make a report, and the Speaker will very expeditiously make a decision about how to proceed."

"Will the Rep be asked to resign?"

"I can't answer that, mostly because I don't know. It's up to the Speaker."

"I don't want to see anyone get fired. I just want a new job."

"Well Jamie, hypothetically, it could go to the ethics committee within the House for disposition."

"So, his peers would decide his fate?"

"That's possible."

"Who chairs the ethics committee?"

"Marty Walsh is the Chairman of the committee."

"Okay, cool."

"The ethics committee can recommend a series of actions, up to expulsion. Then the House members would vote. This is only one example and that it's really too early to tell how this will go."

"There is no way other Reps are going to recommend that he get expelled."

"Jamie, that's ten steps from where we are now."

"Am I culpable because I didn't say no? There were lots of violations, and I didn't say no."

Kennedy and Fleming both spoke up to respond.

Kennedy said, "We are not your personal counsel and that if you wish to speak with your own counsel, you should do so and are free to do so at any time."

Fleming added, "No ethics complaints have been made against you at this point."

Kennedy went on, "There are seven people who know about the investigation: the Representative, the Speaker, Toby, Eisenberg, Dana, me, and you. I have an obligation to report complaints to the Speaker. Never have I reported anything like this in confidence where it has been conveyed to other people. We are respectful of that. We are doing our best to not release information to anyone. Anything from this office will not identify you by name."

"Do I have anything to worry about?"

"I do not have any reason to disbelieve you. The only way you could be in trouble with us is if you've made false allegations. If the Representative were to come back and say, that's not true and here's a stack of documents that shows that it isn't true."

Kennedy goes on to explain, "This isn't a court. The Speaker has ordered me to do this with all deliberate speed, going as fast as we can while maintaining the integrity of the investigation. Going as fast as we can, I'm hoping it's a matter of days. We'll go where the facts lead us. It's a review of facts and an educated guess."

Kennedy added, "Candidly, if I can't determine, pick one allegation – Ken (Simoncini) – if there's nothing to support the fact that Ken is not working, one way or the other, then I will have no basis to conclude one way or the other. I suspect that on any number of these, there will be evidence and that I will be able to make a determination one way or the other."

Kennedy concluded the interview with Ryan by asking her to bring in the pay stubs and to bring him the name of the other aide that she confided in about the picture.

"I want to end on this note. Thank you for coming in and please bear with us while we work through what happened."

"Can I pick up extra shifts at my bartending job?"

"I would advise against doing that during normal business hours while you are on paid administrative leave. But, I don't think you will be on paid administrative leave for very long."

Kennedy and Fleming consulted together over the to-do list and next steps for Ryan including setting the phone message recording, the name of the aide, and the paystubs.

"I would point out that the investigation does not have to be over for you to get a transfer," said Kennedy.

Wednesday, March 13, 2013

Attorney Kennedy had consulted with John Fresolo's attorney, Thomas Kiley, and they agreed to meet for an interview at 4:00 PM on Wednesday, March 13, 2013. This meeting was part of the pre-investigation process that Kennedy had launched at the direction of Speaker DeLeo. The session with Fresolo was only one of many that Kennedy and his associate, Fleming, were conducting with everyone involved in the general matter of allegations that Fresolo's aide had made against him.

It had only been five days since Fresolo had received the devastating phone call from Kennedy notifying him of the seven allegations being made by his aide. Over the weekend, Fresolo had searched for and found some recommendations for legal counsel. He felt lucky that Kiley had agreed to represent him going forward. He didn't know Kiley personally but had a good feeling based on his reputation for handling difficult cases. They had met briefly, and Fresolo knew that his fate was largely in the hands of this stranger.

Fresolo did not know what to expect from this meeting. He had already told Kennedy on the phone last Friday that all of the allegations were nonsense. Now, he would have to go through it all again. Maybe Kennedy would understand better that Ryan was making false claims.

Chief Counsel Jim Kennedy started the interview by thanking Fresolo for coming in and explaining that he didn't want to be here anymore than the Representative did, but that the Speaker had ordered him to conduct this investigation.

Fresolo's attorney, Tom Kiley, spoke up immediately.

"Before we get started, I want it noted that my client has an expectation of privacy. If there has been a violation of his privacy rights, we don't intend to waive any rights here today. If Jamie Ryan did something that she shouldn't have done in terms of access, we are not waiving our rights on that."

Kennedy responded, "Alright, we'll note that. Let me repeat that I started this meeting by saying that I don't want to be here anymore than you do. I hope that in the last fourteen years I've always treated you with respect. There are some difficult questions that I need to ask today, but I am going to do this as respectfully as I can."

Kennedy continued, "First, let me give you a bit of background about how this all came to light. On November 28, 2012, four months ago, Jamie Ryan came to my office (Office of Legal Counsel) and spoke to Paul Iannuccillo. Ryan posed a couple of hypotheticals to Paul. She posed some hypos with Fleming (Deputy Counsel) as well but never made any specific complaints. We told her that she could come back any time she had concerns. We told her the door was open. Four months later, she came back in to discuss the ethics advisory on March 5, 2013. That's when she began to make the initial complaints. We spoke to her yesterday, and she made several additional complaints, which I shared with your attorney."

Atty. Kiley asked, "Are those the things that Jamie had, literally, just added yesterday?"

"Yes."

Fresolo breaks in, "If I could just interrupt and say that Jamie has never said that she is unhappy, and that is the reason I'm so blown away by this."

"John, once an employee comes in and makes an allegation, I have a statutory and ethical obligation to inform the Speaker. I have an ethical obligation to do that as an attorney and a statutory obligation as Counsel to the House. Once I brought this to the attention of the Speaker, he ordered me to investigate, which is why we are here now."

"Listen, John, I have not taken a position on this. I have one half of the story, maybe one and a half parts of the story since we spoke to you on Friday night, but I haven't reached any conclusions."

Kennedy observed he was aware of Fresolo's privileged rights with his attorney.

"As we go through and ask a series of questions, I am advising you that any communications you have had with your attorney are privileged and you are not to tell us about those. If you need a break at any point to consult with your lawyer, you should just let us know."

Kennedy continued, "Further, this meeting is not a deposition, this is not a court, and I am just trying to get to the bottom of what's happened here and make sure that we have as complete and accurate a picture of what happened as we possibly can."

"John, I'm going to start with one of the allegations that have been made. The allegation is that you used your official position and state resources to help your sister avoid jury duty."

"That's just not true. My sister, whose name is Patricia (Tricia) Uwazany, lives in Brimfield, Mass. She received a jury notice to report to Springfield. She called me and said – John I don't know how to get to Springfield, I have never been there. I told her I understood – she's really a Worcester girl, she works in Worcester every day. So, I asked my aide Jamie to call and see if there was a closer courthouse to where Tricia lived. She got back to me and said the closest courthouse was Palmer, but they don't have a jury pool. As it turned out, the jury duty was postponed, but she is again assigned to Springfield. I told her she would have to go.

"Would there be any text messages, emails, or other records between you and Jamie related to your sister's jury duty service?"

"I'm not sure, but there could be emails and text messages that show who initiated contact."

"Do you regularly assist constituents with getting out of jury duty?

"I try to help everyone that calls my office. Jamie may have something to do with that. With a lot of things, Jamie would come to me and suggest things."

"What sort of things would she suggest?"

"I can't remember something right this minute, but it was more like her saying -why don't I do this or that?"

Fresolo expanded on his explanation.

"What happens in a lot of these cases is that Jamie would suggest a course of action. She is very aggressive, and I put a lot of faith in her. That is why I am bewildered. I can't believe this. I've treated her like family."

"Another allegation has been made that you directed Jamie to perform campaign work during normal business hours. Did you ask her to perform campaign work during normal business hours while she is being paid by the House?"

"No, I have never asked her to do campaign work during normal business hours. She has volunteered to do campaign work. Jamie has suggested that she can do campaign work because she lives close to the city in Weymouth."

"How do the conversations about her volunteering to do campaign work come about?"

"I can't say how they come about. She just says that she'll take care of it. But, I have told her that I don't need her help. I have people that can do envelopes. I have one person who does it all the time. She offers to do other things, like, do you want me to stand at a poll on election day? She says she has held signs for others. I told her that I didn't need her for that. To be honest, I think she was trying to get out of work on Election Day by offering to hold signs. She asked me are you backing anyone in the City Council, do you want to get their names? I told her no."

"Has Jamie ever been to Worcester for any of your campaign events?"

"Yes, but I never instructed her to come. My aides know when my functions are, either at night or in the morning. If they want to come, they are more than welcome."

"How many campaign events do you think you have had since Jamie has been with you?"

"I have two campaign events a year, so a total of four campaign events since Jamie started working for me."

"Did Jamie help with any of those events?"

"She took pictures at those events, and if someone came up to me with an issue, I asked her to take notes."

"Can you confirm that none of those events took place during normal business hours?"

"The evening event in March started at 6:00 PM, and the upcoming event in October is a breakfast event."

"Did you mail stamps to Jamie for campaign mailings?"

"I don't have a recollection of mailing her stamps. I have sent her checks for stamps for the office, and she's picked up stamps. She might have picked up stamps for a mailing, but I can't recall."

"Would the stamps have been for a campaign event?"

"It was for a mailing. You are bringing it up, I'm just trying to be honest. I don't recall mailing her stamps."

"Did you instruct Jamie to do the labels for your campaign fundraiser?"

"Jamie has printed labels for me, for mailings, and I have a mailing list."

"Do you use the mailing list for anything other than campaign events?"

"The list is used for campaign events and for Christmas cards."

"Did you instruct Jamie to stuff envelopes for your campaign events?"

"I don't remember Jamie stuffing envelopes for my campaign list."

"Did you instruct Jamie to maintain a campaign mailing list. Is that the list saved on the House LIS system as "Christmas List?"

"Yes, I call it my mailing list. When someone dies, I ask her to update the mailing list."

"How does someone get on the mailing list? Do they have to have donated to your campaign to get on the list?"

"No, people don't have to donate to my campaign to get on the mailing list. It's made up of constituents."

"Is the list saved with the name, Christmas List?"

"It could be, but I'll remind you, I'm computer illiterate. I rely on the aide to do this work. The Christmas List is on the system, but I couldn't find it for you."

"Did you instruct Jamie to work on a campaign for another candidate other than yourself?"

"Absolutely not. She was excited about me endorsing that candidate. People I sat with at her wedding worked on that campaign. These people were her friends. If she said that I forced her to work on that campaign, it is a complete and total lie and exaggeration. I met those girls at the table at her wedding. There were three girls – and at least one of them worked for that campaign."

"Did you tell Jamie that a specific individual from that person's campaign staff would be contacting her with instructions?"

"I could have. I don't know. That staff person is my contact person on that campaign."

"Did Jamie assist in organizing a campaign event with the candidate's wife at a Senior Center in Worcester?"

"It was not a Senior Center. It was the Mount Carmel apartments. I asked her to book the space for that night so that I could go and introduce the candidate's wife. She did set that up. I don't consider that campaign work. I didn't think of that as – an ask – for a campaign-related issue. I would consider it introducing my constituents to a candidate. It wasn't a fundraiser. It was a coffee event."

"Are there any email or text messages that will confirm all this?"

"There could be. I texted Jamie quite a bit. I texted her a lot because she wasn't at her desk a lot. It often happened that I would try to reach her, and she would not be at her desk. I didn't discuss that with her because I didn't want to be a pain in the ass. When I did bring up those sorts of things, she became very defensive. She was a very defensive girl. When you bring something up, she would well-up. I would think that she would consider me to be not a good boss, but a great boss."

"When was the campaign event at the Mount Carmel apartments?"

"It was Monday, March 11."

Kennedy moved on to another of the series of allegations that Fresolo's aide was making against him.

"The allegation is that you directed Jamie to perform personal services during normal business hours, including completing your daughter's college application."

"I have two daughters, Francesca, we call her Frankie and Maria. I asked Jamie to create a resume for Frankie. There might be emails and text messages that would confirm that. My daughter could have called her, or her mother could have emailed Jamie with the information. I don't send emails; I send text messages. I think I told her verbally that my daughter was going to call her with all the relevant information that Jamie would need to create her resume."

"Did you instruct Jamie to help Maria get settled at Worcester State University and then later at Quinsigamond Community College? Did you ask Jamie to contact the housing office at Worcester State?"

"My daughter lives in Worcester with her Mom. She wants to live on campus at Worcester State. It costs $10,000 above the tuition for her to live on campus. I told my daughter you live four miles from there. I told her that she could go and live with her grandmother to be even closer. My daughters are 19 and 20. Neither has ever called my office. But then, my daughter called Jamie and said my father doesn't know I'm calling, but can you look into housing for me to stay in a dorm at Worcester State?"

Fresolo continued, "My daughter told Jamie that I didn't want to pay, but she told Jamie she would pay it herself. She told Jamie she was filling out the application herself and could she help? So, after the call, Jamie tells me, FYI, Maria called. She wants me to look into housing for her at Worcester State. I told Jamie absolutely not. If my daughter wants to do it, she can do it on her own. And, that's when Jamie told me – well, I already helped her fill out her application."

"She told me after the fact. I did not tell her to call housing at Worcester State. I never wanted her to live there."

"Did you instruct Jamie to contact the admissions director at Quinsigamond?

"I may have asked her to do something like that. My daughter wanted a transfer so I asked Jamie to set up a time that I could go with her to Quinsig College. I rely on Jamie for everything. She put the appointment on this phone. She instructed me to get a new phone. I had a flip-up. She said you need to get this and this. I brought a phone, she took it from, I don't know the password, zero, zip. She showed me this is how you get to your calendar; this is how you enter it. So, while we are at Quinsig, I go to the calendar to find out what and where we're supposed to be and who we are supposed to be meeting with. She set up an appointment with my daughter and me. When we were at the college, I asked for the name of the girl Jamie put down, but it was the wrong name. I called Jamie and asked, do you know who I am supposed to meet and asked her to find the right name. No big deal. I don't know who it was we met with. I think it was the admissions director, it was a black woman.

"Are there any emails or text message that will confirm this?"

"Maybe. If it's a violation to contact an admissions director for my daughter, I didn't think it would be a violation."

"Did you ask Jamie to help you get your daughter a job at UMass?"

"Yes. No."

Attorney Kiley commented on the conflicting answers and asked if Fleming, who was taking notes if she caught it in the notes?"

"Yes, Jamie did assist in setting up a time for her to meet with someone at UMass. I went to the Albie Sherman (building) opening. I talked to a guy who sets up and breaks down the event space. I said I'm trying to find my daughter a job. She doesn't mind working weekends. The guy said he was looking for people to breakdown, setup, etc. He also said that if it's a woman, she can clean bathrooms."

"Can you clarify who it was you spoke to, and how was the job connected to UMass? How did that work?"

"I think his name was Anthony. I told Jamie to send Frankie's resume to him. She was going to be paid per diem. I think it was on a per diem job."

"Are you still trying to get your daughter a job at UMass?"

"The guy Anthony was a UMass employee. Frankie got a job off Craigslist at the Doubletree in Westborough. But she still hopes that UMass will call her back for work on the weekends. UMass told her that they would be calling her sometime in March. So far, still no phone call."

"Would you say it was unusual or not for members of your family to call Jamie directly?"

"No, it was not unusual, they did that."

Kennedy moved on to an allegation that involved speeding tickets that his sister, Sandy, had received.

"Did you direct Jamie to assist your Sister in appealing two speeding tickets?"

"My sister, Sandy Skrzek, lives in Worcester but is not a constituent because she does not live in my district. I have only just heard about this from Tom, not you. Tom told me that Sandy called with two speeding tickets. This is the first I've heard of it."

"Are there any emails or texts that will confirm this information?"

Attorney Kiley responded, "There were not any emails on this subject until today. I can confirm there are two outstanding tickets, one for Sandy and one for her husband. I can provide the ticket docket numbers."

"That won't be necessary at this time."

Kennedy brought up the next allegation about helping his niece, Amy, get a job at the Attorney General's office.

"Did you direct Jamie to assist your niece in obtaining a job in the Attorney General's office?"

"My niece Amy told me she had applied for a job at Attorney General Coakley's office. In my view, Amy was a very qualified candidate. I saw Martha Coakley and asked if I could call her about it. The Attorney General said – let me see if I can get her an interview."

Fresolo continued, "My niece called me between two and four weeks later to say – Uncle John, I haven't heard anything yet. I asked Jamie to call the AG's office and ask if they had started interviews. I take that back, maybe she had the interview already, she didn't hear back. I instructed Jamie to make a call to see if they had picked someone or if the job was still available. Jamie told me she spoke to someone at the AG's office who said they are about to pick the candidate and that my niece did very well."

Fresolo added, "My niece works in the Worcester office. She has since moved to Waltham but is still employed by the AG. I think she holds the position of investigator, but I'm not sure. Whatever position she holds, she has held it for over a year."

"Did you ask Jamie to write a letter of recommendation for your niece and to get you time with the AG's office?"

"I could have."

"Did you ask Jamie to walk your niece over to the interview?"

"No. If she did that she did it on her own. This is the first I heard of it. I'm kind of floored when I hear that. She might have gotten Amy a parking spot. I thought maybe that was the next thing you were going to ask."

"Did the AG call your office to tell you that Amy had gotten the job?"

"I don't recall the AG calling to say that Amy had gotten the job."

Kennedy introduced the allegation that Fresolo had directed his aide to assist his nephew, Nick, in obtaining a job at DOT (Department of Transportation).

"Did you direct Jamie to assist your nephew in obtaining a job at the DOT?"

"My nephew is a seasonal summer worker for the DOT. This is a laborer position for summer help. The DOT had said they were going to call him back for more work this year. My sister-in-law (Anita) was anxious and wanted to make sure they hadn't overlooked him or forgotten about him. She wanted to get an application. That was the basis of the email that Jamie saw. I told Jamie to talk to Donnie Daily about it. Jamie told my sister-in-law about where to find the application."

"John, would you explain specifically what you asked her to do?"

"Don Daily is a liaison for DOT. He's in the building a lot. He comes into my office all the time. Jamie takes it upon herself to ask him about jobs. She said to him – we need to get the Rep's nephew a job. She took control."

"What exactly did you ask Jamie to do?"

"I asked her to get him an application. And then I spoke to them. I asked DOT why they didn't want to hire him. They said it was because of the press. I said the press will be my problem. If anyone is going to get bad press about this, it will be me. They finally gave him a job. Last summer, I called for my daughter, Francesca, and she didn't get the position because of her last name. She was counting on it. Her cousin was working there, and she wanted to work there too. She was really disappointed, and she let me know about it."

Fresolo continued, "My sister-in-law contacted Jamie without my knowing about it. My sister-in-law told Jamie she was having trouble getting an application. She told Jamie that she wanted to make sure he has income and something to do this summer."

Attorney Kiley spoke up to explain that the email referred to earlier was between the Rep's sister-in-law, Anita, and Jamie.

Fresolo added, "Jamie forwarded it to me. It was initiated by Anita, my sister-in-law, who asked if Jamie could help them get the application in earlier this year because last year it was kind of last minute."

"After you received the FYI from Jamie, what happened next?"

"I told her to speak to Donnie Daily about it. Jamie would take a huge amount of control and had a lot of aggressiveness. That's the way it's been there ever since she started working. I don't know if she spoke to Donny. I don't know if the application has gone out."

"Are there any emails or text messages that will reflect all this?"

"There could be text messages. I responded to the email. I don't know if I deleted that email and just talked to her. But I do know that my sister-in-law emailed her about a summer position again. She couldn't get an application. Jamie sent her the application in an email. She did do that; I know that much."

Kennedy then brought up the next allegation.

"Did you direct Jamie to assist your uncle, Richard, in obtaining a job at a private company?"

"Yes, I initially made the call to Diamond Chevrolet. That never transpired because the owner never called me back. I asked Jamie to call Elder Services of Worcester. They got back to her and said they didn't have anything. I asked her to contact a lobbyist for the new dealers to see if they are looking for drivers. After a couple calls to the lobbyist, I probably texted Jamie to see if there was any response from him yet. Jamie would have made repeated calls. The lobbyist told us to have Richard go down to see so and so and let me know when he goes down. My uncle fell and hurt himself and never went. He never got a job. There would be a text on that."

Kennedy reviewed the next allegation that the Representative directed Ryan to call NSTAR to ensure his brother's plumbing business, Fresolo Plumbing, was placed on NSTAR's preferred vendor list.

"The plumbing company is owned by my brother, Rocky and his son Rocky, Jr. Rocky Jr. had contacted me initially. He said I just did a job for this woman and she wanted to hire us but couldn't because we're not on NSTAR's preferred list. He asked me if I knew how to get on the list. I told Jamie that exact scenario and told her to call NSTAR and see if he can point us in the right direction. There's probably a text or voice message asking her to check on this. She sent me the email correspondence. The person she spoke with at NSTAR said give me his name and so and so will call him by the end of the week. By the end of the week, there was no call. I told Jamie it's the end of the week and Rocky Jr. still hadn't heard. So, I asked Jamie to call back. NSTAR said he'll get a call today. Next thing I see NSTAR tells Jamie to tell the Rep that he is on the list. I saw my brother at a funeral later, and he came over and said thank you for helping him get on the preferred list."

"Do you have any direct financial interest or ownership stake in the plumbing company?"

"I'm not a plumber. I have no financial interest in my brother's plumbing company."

"When did this happen?"

"This happened a few weeks ago. Rocky Jr. had called and given Jamie whatever information she needed to make those calls. I think I gave Jamie his cell phone number. No. I think I gave Jamie my brother's cell phone number and he must have given her Rocky Jr.'s number."

Kennedy turned to the next allegation about employment recommendations.

"Did you direct Jamie to apply pressure in connection with certain recommendations for employment?"

"I told Jamie when I interviewed her, I pointed to the door and said see where it says State Rep, it should say employment agency. I told her four out of five calls that come into my office are job-related. I asked her, are you going to have a problem with that? She said no, she wouldn't have a problem. It's not uncommon for an urban district."

Kennedy and Fresolo commiserated about the number of calls that come in from people who are looking for work, particularly in urban districts.

"Jamie gets the calls; they call the office. Or, if I see them on the street, I tell them to send it into the office. I ask her to find a point person, and I ask her to call on their behalf. If that's illegal, I never knew it was. It was done with sincerity trying to help people."

Fresolo continued, "I asked her to follow up on things. At the state hospital, they were supposed to hire 100 people. I talked to a DMH staff person. I asked him would you mind if I send some people your way for jobs. He said absolutely, send all the entry-level positions, send them to Worcester Recovery Center. That's just one instance. I'll say to Jamie, let's call UMass Memorial. A contact of mine there always tells me if there are good people out there looking for jobs, he wants to know."

"After you make a recommendation, did you have a policy with her about how and when she was to follow-up? Did you instruct her to follow-up a certain number of times?"

"No, I'd say can I have an update on our constituent issues? If I haven't heard anything, I'd say call and see if they are interviewing yet? If someone were told two weeks ago that they would hear something and they hadn't heard yet, I'd tell her to call and check. I'd have to remind her to do these things. If I didn't remember, it didn't get done. I talked to her about this, and she got defensive. She didn't do anything; she didn't have very much work to do. There were days I came in; I didn't ask her to do anything."

Kennedy then asked Fresolo if he had talked to Ryan about the recent ethics advisory opinion on ethics.

"I gave Jamie the handout from the caucus. I told her we can't write letters of recommendation anymore. I said read it, from what I heard at the caucus, I think that's what this means. I told her to make sure and read this. I haven't signed a recommendation letter since the caucus in February. Instead, I instructed Jamie to make follow-up phone calls and to make verbal recommendations for people."

"I'd like to clarify and confirm that you have made verbal recommendations since the advisory came out, just not written ones?"

"Yes, absolutely. If we get a call, I'm telling Jamie that so-and-so has an interview next Tuesday and that she needs to follow-up. For example, I'm trying to get someone a kitchen job at Worcester State Hospital. I asked her to call and follow-up."

Kennedy paused the interview to discuss the ethics advisory and its intent. They discussed the ethics training that is coming up on March 21. Kennedy went on to advise that the Representative is not banned from making written recommendations and that making oral recommendations may be more problematic than making written ones. Kennedy offered to discuss and clarify the advisory with Fresolo off-line once they finished this matter.

Kennedy then brought up the next allegation.

"Have you directed Jamie to contact TD Bank North to obtain concert tickets?"

"Yes, I have."

"Who is your contact at the bank?"

"My contact is Richard Krezwick. He was the GM of the Centrum in Worcester for five or six years. When he moved to TD Bank North, when the Garden opened, he gave me his card. He said if you ever need anything, call me. In the two years, Jamie has worked for me, she has called five to six times, tops. Mostly for the same guy and one time for his brother. George Panagiotou and his brother Matthew. These are my good friends."

"What is the arrangement?"

"When you buy them that way over the phone with a credit card, they charge you a service fee. Whatever that fee is, that is what I charge my good, good friends, who I have known my whole adult life. She knows that they are my good friends, so the fee charge is just whatever I have paid."

"Have you directed Jamie to charge certain people whom you do not know all that well an upcharge and explain that the extra amount being charged as part of the fee for obtaining the tickets?"

"No. Mathew called her recently and said I charged him too much. The tickets were for a niece or nephew for the Justin Bieber concert, I think. Matthew calls her says to Jamie, the girl says the tickets only amount to this much, but she was charged this much, and Jamie asked me about it. Jamie never touches the tickets, they go to my house, so she doesn't know about the service fee. She asks me for the number of my personal debit card when I buy the tickets."

"So, Matthew asks you to get tickets to a Justin Bieber concert, which is a young kid's concert?"

"Yes. He called and asked for it – please, John – can you get them. I don't like calling. I didn't know if it was legal or illegal, I just told her to do it. She did it like that, no problem. I instructed her to call the Garden. There was an additional charge for the service fee. I gave the tickets to Matthew. Next day, Matthew calls Jamie and asks Jamie why there's a difference between the face value of the tickets and the total amount paid."

"Why would your friend Matthew call Jamie about the tickets instead of calling you directly?"

"Matthew may have called her initially. I might have instructed Matthew to call Jamie at the office and tell her what concert you want. I paid the service charge. I collected the cash from him. He came to my house to pick up the tickets. There were four tickets."

"Are there any emails or text messages that would reflect this?"

"There are no emails or text messages on this. George has called me four times. I went to the Eagles once. Matthew other times, other than Justin Bieber. I would think that I've gotten tickets six times total, in that range. I did it for myself three times, I took my daughters to a Boston Celtics game. I don't remember if it was when Jamie worked there or not. I went to Barry Manilow and to the Eagles. I've been three times since I've been a Rep. I never bought tickets for someone I didn't know."

Kennedy then relayed the next allegation that Fresolo employs a staff person who has not appeared for work for many months, has no email address, and whose pay stubs are delivered to Fresolo.

"Jamie has alleged that your staff person is not working here. She gets his pay stubs and has given them to you in the past, and now apparently she keeps them in a drawer?"

"Jamie used to give the pay stubs to me."

"I have Ken Simoncini's pay stubs going back for several months."

Fresolo reviewed the stack of paystubs placed on the table by Kennedy.

"So, that's why they stopped. She has the paystubs. She used to give them to me. For some reason, they stopped. That's why I haven't seen one in a while. She used to leave it in my district envelope with mine and then I would leave it under his windshield wiper where his car was parked in his driveway. This is an example of where Jamie just does what she does."

"How is it that you know Ken Simoncini?"

"Ken is an adult friend for 20 years. He is a close, loyal friend and supporter but not a supporter, in politics."

"Are you neighbors at 24 Dolly Drive and 25 Dolly Drive in Worcester?"

"How did you find that out?"

"We did our own independent research on Ken. Is he your Accountant?"

"He's not my campaign treasurer. He does my personal taxes. He doesn't do my OCPF (Office of Campaign and Political Finance)."

"I notice that Ken has donated to your campaign pretty consistently over the last decade."

"He comes to my parties. He'll hold a sign. He's 70 years old. I haven't had a race in a while."

"Where does Ken work?"

"Ken has his own business."

"No, that's not what I mean. Where does Ken work for the House? Do you have a district office?"

"Ken covers district hours. He comes with me when I need him. I had a district office, but I closed it four or five years ago because people weren't coming in."

"Where does Ken work?"

"I don't have a district office."

"Well, then how many hours per week does Ken work for you?"

"It differs. Some weeks, 10 hours, some he works 20-25 hours. He worked for me for four to five years, then stopped for a while because he didn't have time to do it. He started with me about 10 years ago. He has been working for me, since he started again, about four to five years now."

"What work does he perform for you?"

"He covers the office hours. He goes to meetings I can't attend. He takes care of district issues. He is my district aide."

"How do you communicate with Ken?"

"On the phone or verbally."

"How come Ken doesn't have a State House email address or a user account?"

"No one has ever asked him to. It's not needed for me. I don't do things on email. He lives across the street."

"If you call your district office number, does Ken pick up the phone?"

"You would get my name. He has access to retrieve my messages. I give him the messages from my answering machine. It's through Verizon. The message says if you'd like to reach me in Boston, please dial 617-722-2360."

"How come Jamie has never met Ken? How is it that they have never worked on a constituent matter together?"

"Never met Ken? That's not true. Jamie talked to Ken as recently as last week about a tax question. She took it upon herself to call him. This is what is so mind-boggling about all of this."

"Our House records indicate that Ken earns $15,024.61, which is half time or 18.75 hours per week."

"If that's what it says, that's what it says."

Fresolo elaborated on Ken's behavior, stating that he came to the ethics courses that were required and that Jamie set up a parking spot for him.

"Yes, we see that Ken has completed his training requirements. We will backtrack to see if we can confirm the parking spot around that time."

"Have you spoken to Ken about any of these allegations?"

"I told him about the allegations. I told him that Jamie said he didn't exist. For some reason, she takes exception to the fact that I have a district aide. She doesn't think he does much for the money he gets paid, but that's not her business. I handle my district office and my district. I said to him the allegation I have a district aide who doesn't work."

"What did Ken say in response to you?"

"Ken asked, what's that all about?"

"Did you instruct Ken to cooperate with the investigation?"

"Yes."

"I called Ken and asked him to come in for an interview, but he refused."

"I know that you called him. There is no way I can break down and force the guy to come in. He's a grown man. He offered to resign on the spot. He told me I could have the job if I want. He said the job is not important to him. After April 15 Ken could be available at your beck and call, but right now he has clients, and he can't come in."

"John, this request is not a request, it's not discretionary."

"Ken cannot get away in the middle of tax season. He can't do it."

"Let me be frank. Ken needs to get to a good place with me by five o'clock tomorrow. He needs to agree to a time he can be interviewed. I'm willing to be flexible within reason but that I need to see him by the end of the week."

"If you want to fire him, fire him. He's a grown man. I can't control him. He told me to take the job, the $14 thousand is not worth it. He said he hadn't caused this. He was hot with me. I'm sure he was hot with you too."

Attorney Kiley interjected that perhaps the meeting could be conducted with Ken over the phone.

Kennedy said, "It needs to be a face to face meeting. I need to see Ken."

Fresolo offered, "Ken works on Boston Turnpike Road in Shrewsbury from morning until night, and perhaps House Counsel could go out to see him there."

Fleming spoke up to ask, "Is there anywhere else we can look for a record of Ken's work for the House?"

"I can't think of any other records or any other place that House Counsel could look for records to demonstrate the work that Ken performs for the House."

Fleming asked, "When are your office hours?"

"I don't hold office hours through the winter. The *Worcester Telegram* no longer prints the office hours in a timeframe that makes sense, so I don't hold office hours in the winter anymore. I go to places and tell people about it. Ken comes with me to Dunkin Donuts. That's something I don't discuss with Jamie. I don't have to answer to her."

Kennedy next reviewed an allegation that Fresolo had filed inaccurate per diem reports greatly inflating the number of trips made to the State House.

"In 2011 did you report that you were here at the State House 218 days?"

Attorney Kiley spoke up at this point and handed Kennedy and Fleming a copy of a *Worcester Telegram* article with a headline that read: Fresolo makes the top 10 list for travel payments.

Kiley said, "Jamie saw this article like everyone else, and she is just repeating what she read in the newspaper."

Fresolo added, "I saw the report and believe the number of trips was 211 and not 218 because when I saw it, I remember thinking they didn't have the number right."

Kennedy continued, "Will your Easy-Pass Fast-Lane reflect your trips?"

Kiley responded, "Those records won't match the Rep's per diems because he used to travel in with John Binienda, and they split the driving."

Fresolo added, "As it is, I haven't driven in with Binienda in about six months."

Kennedy continued, "Jamie claims that you are only here for formal sessions and that you very rarely attend committee hearings."

"I'm here."

"Is there anyone we could speak with to establish that you attend the HWM (House Ways and Means) meetings?"

"I don't know of anyone."

Kennedy turns the interview to the next allegation and prefaces his questions by stating that everyone is sorry that there is a need to have this discussion.

"It's not something we want to talk about."

Attorney Kiley said, "To the extent, we have privacy issues, the Representative is not waiving any of his rights."

Fresolo spoke up, "Can I stop you there? I wouldn't even know how to direct her to log onto Facebook through my House email. Jamie is the one who put me on Facebook. I don't know anything about it. I did not direct her to log onto it through email. This is just absolutely wrong. She wanted me on Facebook. She told me it was a good way of staying updated and keeping current. I saw that everyone else was doing it, so I said okay."

Fresolo continued, "Before Jamie worked for me, I had no Facebook presence whatsoever. Jamie offered to create an account. Shortly after she came to work for me. I don't know how long I've been on Facebook. It's been a year or two on Facebook. Jamie set up the account."

Fresolo became equivocal about his recollection of when he started using Facebook.

"It's possible that before Jamie, Paul (previous aide) set up Facebook, I don't think so, I'm not sure. Whoever set it up, told me I should be on Facebook. It's a new fad. It's how you keep your name out there. I use Facebook at home and through my phone."

Kennedy produced a copy of a Facebook page and showed it to Fresolo.

"Is this a page from your Facebook account?"

"Yes. These are my messages."

"Is this a page you use for personal and political purposes?"

"I use it for personal use. Let me be perfectly clear. I have never asked to be friends with anyone. The only way I'm friends with people is that they ask me, and I confirm. I very seldom confirm unless they are from Worcester. I look, I click on it to see where they are from. If it isn't Worcester and it isn't someone I know, then I am not friends with them. I have never asked anyone to be my friend.

Fresolo looked over the Facebook page more closely and acknowledged that he had dated the woman named on the message for a few months.

"Who has access to your Facebook page?"

"I thought it was only me. I thought her access was limited. You have to click on the messages to read the messages. I won't do that shit again, but I did not think that she could see it."

Fresolo tried to demonstrate how he can access messages through his phone, showing Kennedy his phone.

"I thought Jamie's access was limited to posting pictures on it. I gave her permission to access my Facebook page and post photos. Since she has worked for me, she has put up my endorsement of another political candidate, my chairing of a meeting, etc. Now I see everyone else posting things on Facebook, so I told Jamie to do it too. The last photo she posted was of a marine who received a high honor, and I was there to give him the citation, so I asked her to post that."

At this point in the interview, a discussion began about how instant messaging works on Facebook and whether those messages automatically appear on a computer screen when someone else logs in through the Representative's account or whether the person who is logged on through the computer must click on the messages to open them.

"She must have had to click on the messages to view them, and this is a violation of my privacy."

Fresolo acknowledges that he sent messages on the printout. One message was on March 6 at 3:17 PM. Another message was on Thursday, March 7, at 11:23 AM. A third message was Friday, March 8, at 7:32 AM.

Fresolo noted that there was an earlier part of the conversation from January 2 that does not appear in the printout.

"I didn't see the January 2 message until January 5 at which point I wrote – call me back. I sent the message to her on January 5, which was a Saturday, at 9:55 PM."

"I never shut off my computer. I never shut that thing off. Jamie has no business hitting that icon or opening up any messages."

"When was the last time you accessed your Facebook page from your office?"

"It could have been last Wednesday (March 5). I was here (Boston) last Wednesday. I could have. I very seldom go on Facebook on that computer. Here is what I recall Wednesday. I started opening my mail. She came in, and she wanted to talk to me about something. There's a job in the Labor and Workforce Committee. She said it's a research analyst."

Jamie said, "I want to apply for it. Do you have a problem with that?"

"No."

"You don't mind?"

"I don't mind."

"You don't?"

Fresolo said she seemed surprised. He continued, "I said to her I would never stop you from bettering yourself."

Fresolo stated that it was like she was pissed that I wasn't upset she was interviewing for another job.

"This is the make-up of her."

Fresolo then explained that he was to meet later that day with Thomas Conroy, Chairman of the Labor and Workforce

Committee. Jamie indicated to him that she was interviewing coincidentally at the same time.

"Would you put in a good word to Chairman Conroy?"

"Yes, I will."

Fresolo then described to Kennedy the discussion he had with Conroy about his possible role on the committee.

Fresolo explained that he told Conroy, "I didn't ask for this committee."

Fresolo described more of the conversation topics with Conroy, including he's never been offered a chairmanship, and it's a disgrace that Representative Miceli is assigned to sit in a cubicle.

At this point, Attorney Kiley advised Fresolo to get back on point.

"As it turned out, Jamie's application for a research position never came up. I forgot all about it until I got back to the State House. Jamie asked me about the meeting, and I told her I had forgotten to mention her. She looked like she wanted to kill me."

Fresolo added that Jamie worked from home on Thursday, March 7 due to the weather. "As far as I knew she was planning to be working the week of March 11."

Returning to the topic of when he last used Facebook, Fresolo stated he could have accessed it on Wednesday, March 8.

"That could be the reason that the message appears on the page. I don't know if Jamie still has my password. I don't even know my password on Facebook. She put it all in and set it all up."

"Did you give Jamie your Facebook password?"

"Yes, she's got it. But that's not right that she clicks the message. The messages don't stay open. They don't stay open. I'm not arguing. Look at the time. It's before eight o'clock in the morning. I wonder if she came to the House Counsel on Friday, did she click open the messages because she was looking to find something? I only suggest that."

"I would suggest that you change the Facebook password."

Attorney Kiley laughs, "We've been trying to change the password."

"I had no knowledge that she could see my messages. I would never expose anyone to that."

Attorney Kiley spoke up, "What we should all come away with is that this was just stupidity, stupid sexting stupidity."

Fresolo interjected, "I have told two people about these allegations who are dear friends, and they both said the only way she can get this information is because she has my password and that I need to change my password."

"I would advise you to call LIS at the State House tomorrow and change your passwords. You will want to change your password."

Attorney Kiley asks, "Where is this information going to go because we are concerned about this woman's privacy too."

"Right now, the information is internal and has been shared with a very limited number of people. Where else it goes is to be determined. As far as I know with the email, we are the only ones who have custody."

Attorney Kiley said, "We do not deny that this occurred, and we think it should be private."

Fresolo said, "I never knew that my Facebook account is connected to the State House. Everything is so innocent here. Jamie's on a mission to get me, and it's not right."

Kennedy then recounted the next allegation that the Representative used his House email account to send or attempt to send nude photographs of his genitalia to a female who is not the complaining witness. At this point, Kennedy passed out a copy of the picture.

"Have you ever used your House of Representative's email account intentionally or not to send an inappropriate image?"

"I've used texts to message. She texts me; I text her. I have never sent inappropriate images through email. I sent messages through the text on my phone. That's how it was back and forth."

Kennedy points to the page and states this is a snapshot of your sent items from your email. Fresolo looked and found the date it was sent, November 15, 2012.

"It's got to have a time. It was done at my house. Late at night. I remember this picture. This picture is of me. I sent it to this woman (Jane Doe)."

"You intended to text it to her?"

"Yes, I did text it to her.

Attorney Kiley asks Fresolo to see if he can pull up the text from November.

"I don't even know if I still have her in my phone. It was a text from her cell phone. Let me see if I even have her on the phone. Jamie did something to get that image onto his email."

Fresolo found Jane Doe's name and contact information on his phone but does not find the text he sent her with the picture attached.

"May I have (Jane Doe's) last name?"

Attorney Kiley interjects, "We object to putting her name on the record. The woman knows nothing about this and is separated."

Fresolo did not give Kennedy the name or contact information.

Attorney Kiley added, "We don't deny sending her this. This is where it went to her mobile. It says (Jane Doe). It's a phone to phone communication."

Kiley pointed to a screenshot of the Representative's email.

Kennedy responds to correct Kiley, "This is a picture of your sent items in your email."

"That photo was never on my computer like that."

At this point, Fresolo asked – if we can put the picture away? Kennedy turns the paper over.

Kennedy continues about the emails.

"How do you ask Jamie to review emails, what is your general practice?"

"I leave messages up for Jamie to review. When she sees them, she knows that she needs to respond to them. She does it by me, or she sends them from her. She responds. I used to leave them up for her, but that got to be too much. Mainly now, it's on my phone. The messages were staying up there too long. Now, she showed me how to forward them to her. So, I forward it to her and ask her to send a response. Please respond in agreement or something like that."

"Does Jamie respond to emails in your name from your account?"

"Sometimes, yes."

Kennedy addressed the issue of confidentiality.

"Who else did you speak to after we talked on Friday (March 8) beside your attorney?"

"Some friends. They don't work for the State."

"I spoke to Sheila Trapasso of Worcester, William Breault of Worcester, Francis Ford of Paxton, and Ken Simoncini."

"I've done nothing wrong intentionally."

"John, I hope you will trust me to do my job."

Kennedy concludes the interview and agrees he will be in contact with Fresolo and Kiley.

Friday, March 15, 2013

Ken Simoncini worked as an aide to John Fresolo for many years. There was a break in his service at one point, but when it was possible for him to return, he took up as John's district aide. The part-time position provides Representatives with an aide that is dedicated to the local district and generally lives there as well. The aides that work for Representatives in Boston are not necessarily from the Representative's hometown. They generally live closer to Boston as their role is to help at the Representative's main office in the State House. Many of the district aides work from home if the Representative doesn't fund a local office location from his or her own resources. The state does not provide Representatives with a local office.

Kennedy opened the meeting by asking, "Ken, do you know why you are here?"

"I know that you are investigating John for whatever reason. I drove in today with John, and we talked about it on the way in. We did not delve into all the allegations. I know that his aide is making allegations about his per diem and about me being a no-show employee."

Ken continued, "I made John drive me in today and show me where to go. I don't know where his office is. I apologize for the way I spoke to you previously."

"I understand and accept your apology. I don't often call district aides and require them to come to the State House on 48 hours' notice, but this is a serious matter, so I thank you for the apology and for coming in."

"It all worked out, I just had to move around some of my clients."

"Did you say anything to John when he informed you of the allegations?"

"I basically just listened. As far as being a no-show employee, here is a package from your office, which contains my completed ethics training."

"We'll get into that, but I want to discuss the paystubs first. The Representative's other aide brought in all the paystubs back through several months."

"Oh, I didn't think much about why they were never mailed to my house. In the past, the paystubs went to my office. I do get my W-2 form in the mail."

"Have you gotten your W-2 form recently?"

"Yes, I have and as you can see the envelope mailed to me from the House Counsel's office containing the ethics summary. I got this from your office at the end of December. I attended training back in September or August. I attended over at Ashburton. I marked a spot in my appointment book. I believe the training was on August 29. This year I did the ethics class online. I printed out the certificate of completion and sent it to Jamie."

Kennedy said, "Let's back up for a second. How did you come to meet the Representative?"

"I met John 22 years ago. I bought a house on Dolly Drive. I was there a few years before he moved in. Since then we've been close friends."

"How long have you worked for him as an employee of the House?"

"There was a point in time when I started working as the Representative's aide. Don't ask me dates. I worked for him for a while. Then they took the position away and then when the position came back to him he asked me if I wanted to be his aide in Worcester again. I said yes, it was four or five years ago that I came back."

"How many years have you worked for the Representative in total?"

"I think I probably joined the Rep in his second term, and I took a few years break when the House took the position away. I will have to check the records to confirm how long I have worked for the Rep."

"What do you do for work?"

"I'm self-employed."

Ken then started to describe his accounting business.

"No, I meant what work do you perform for the Representative?"

"Oh, I apologize, I didn't realize that."

Kennedy moves on to understand Ken's role better.

"Where do you work for the Representative?"

"My office is in my home. I go wherever the Rep wants to send me. I go with him to meetings. If he can't attend, I go in his place. That's it. Some of the places he holds office hours include Oakhill, Quinsigamond, Addison Apartments. These events are usually held at night in the district."

"Do you have an office you report to?"

"No, it's either at my house or his house. There is no office."

"What does a typical day look like and what duties do you usually perform for the Representative?"

"The Rep calls me and usually asks me to go for office hours or to attend a meeting at the Worcester Public Library. There is no typical day. I'm at his beck and call. When I took this job, I told him that the only time I can't be at your beck and call is February 1 through April 15."

Fleming interjected, "Do you perform any work for the Representative during your busy tax season from February 1 through April 15?"

"No, I don't."

"Do you take any other blocks of time off during the rest of the year?"

"Oh yeah, when I go away up to Hampton Beach for a week in August. This is my vacation week."

Kennedy followed up, "On average, how many hours do you work for the House each week?"

"On average, I work 10 hours a week. Whenever he needs me. He needs me to do something, I go do it. I don't keep track of that stuff."

"You are being paid for 18.75 hours of work per week."

"Well, whatever, it's a part-time thing."

Kennedy noted, "With not working for 10 weeks during tax season plus one week of vacation you would actually have to work much more than 18.75 hours per week to make up for the difference."

"I told the Rep from the beginning that I wouldn't be able to work at all from February 1 through April 15. I make my entire annual income during those 10 weeks."

Ken restates his weekly estimate, "I work anywhere from between eight and 25 hours a week. I do whatever the Rep wants. It could be holding office hours; it could be bringing a citation to someone in a nursing home."

"How do you and the Representative communicate?"

"I communicate with the Rep by telephone, or I just go and knock on his front door."

"Why don't you have a House email account?"

"I didn't know I needed an email. I only use email for my business. My clients email me materials and forms they get in the mail. I don't set up appointments through email. My clients have to call me, and I write the appointment in my appointment book."

"Have you ever written a letter of recommendation or handled any other constituent matter?"

"I don't write letters of recommendation or make phone calls on behalf of constituents."

"Do you do any campaign work for the Representative?"

"No. I don't do campaign work. I don't even hold a sign for him."

"Do you serve as his campaign accountant?"

"I do look over the reports. I make sure everything is done properly. That is my forte."

"Does the Representative have any other accountants?"

"I helped the Rep find someone who did his last OCPF report, but that guy who was doing it died. I helped the campaign treasurer put the report together. The other accountant did the pre-primary before he died. He died in November. I had to call down to the political finance department to find out what was being done because I had no idea. I did all the accounting for John. I helped with the last one because we only had five days to pull it together. I did his year-end report."

"I would like to confirm that you prepared the Representative's year-end report?"

"I helped prepare it."

"Did you receive a payment as the Representative's accountant?"

"I didn't charge. I was not paid. I don't know whether this was right or wrong, but I did not charge."

"Do you have access to the Representative's email or Facebook?"

"I'm not on Facebook, and I don't know how to use it. My wife is on Facebook, but I am not. My wife does not have access to the Rep's Facebook account."

"Have you had any contact with Jamie?"

"She called me about three weeks ago about a constituent of John's who had a problem with his state tax return. I didn't return her call. I was busy. I just didn't have time. I wasn't going to answer a question about a constituent's state tax return when I was up to my ears in my own business. I didn't call her back. I wrote the note down, but then I threw it out."

Ken continued, "I've had conversations with her before. This past August, I took those online ethics. I had to call Jamie to get the website from her so that I could do the training. This past August 2012, I copied the ethics online training completion certificate and gave it to Jamie."

"In total, how many times have you spoken to Jamie?"

"A half dozen times. I met her a couple times at the Rep's events."

"How often did you speak to Jamie's predecessor?"

"I don't know. I don't have any real conversations with John's aides. They have had my number and can call if they need to. One prior aide, Paul, called me a few times. I've only talked to Jamie two or three times. Never exchanged emails with me. I've only met her a couple of times in Worcester. Never met her here in the State House."

"Do you fill out time-sheets?"

"No one has ever asked me to fill out timesheets."

"How do you get your paystubs?"

"They usually go to John's office and then they would come to me."

"When they stopped coming you didn't inquire as to why they stopped?"

"I never called HR. When they stopped coming, I never thought anything of it. I didn't even ask the Rep about it. He would put it on my car under the windshield wiper."

"Did you notice that you weren't getting your State Retirement Board statements?"

"I was surprised by that because they usually mail those to me. The only paperwork that went to John's office was the paystub."

Kennedy shows Ken the stack of paystubs. "These appear to be paystubs for about six months."

He showed Ken the 2010 Statement from the Retirement Board.

Ken asks, "How did Jamie get that? Jamie wasn't even working for John in 2010?"

Kennedy explained, "There is a lag time in terms of when the retirement board notices go out."

Ken responds, "The paystubs weren't something I worried about. I worry about my own business. This is something I do for John. I like doing it. It's a good fit for John and me. I don't worry about little things like this, paystubs."

Ken added, "I'm positive that the W-2s come to my office or house."

"I would expect an accountant to watch out for his W-2, so that doesn't surprise me."

Kennedy turned his question toward Ken's accounting business.

"Tell me about your accounting business."

"I have my own job, my accounting business. It's called Ken Simoncini. I have been semi-retired for the last several years. I've been in the tax business for 50 years. Years ago, I did anything, bookkeeping, financial statements, etc. Now, I only do personal taxes and have gotten rid of all my corporate clients."

Kennedy commented that considering Ken was semi-retired, his schedule was "pretty well packed" with meetings all day long.

"I guess I was surprised that you describe retirement as having meetings all day."

Fleming spoke up and asked, "Are there weeks, outside of tax season from February 1 through April 15, and outside of your weeks' vacation in August when you perform no work for the Representative?"

"If he's got nothing going on, then it could be that I wouldn't work. I'm at his beck and call. He's my boss."

Fleming continued, "Are there any other records we could look at that would show the work you performed for the House?"

"No, there are no other records. Again, I communicate by telephone."

Kennedy asked, "How often do you speak with the Representative by phone? How many times a week does this happen?"

"It may happen a couple of times a month. I sometimes communicate with the Rep by knocking on his door. I could have telephone calls with the Rep as often as once a day, but the calls are sometimes personal."

"Are you the Representative's personal accountant?"

"Yes, I am. I don't charge him for my accounting services. Mainly I don't charge him because he's a friend."

Ken laughed and said, "That's why I only have three friends."

"Would you be willing to sign an affidavit stating that you work the requisite number of hours for your salary?"

"I don't have a problem with that."

"You will need to take the affidavit to an attorney and review with counsel before signing. I want to advise you that it could lead to criminal charges and the loss of your pension."

At this point, Fleming and Jim Kennedy stepped out to finish preparing the affidavit. Upon returning with the document, Kennedy advised Ken that he should seek counsel before signing the affidavit.

Ken read it over and said, "I think the affidavit looks okay."

"I'm not asking you to talk to a lawyer, I am telling you that you need to talk to a lawyer before signing."

Kennedy and Simoncini agree they will talk the following week and that he will have a response on whether he intends to sign the affidavit by Tuesday, March 19.

With that understanding, the interview concluded.

Friday, March 15, 2013

Cindy Trabucco, Staff Director for Chairman Strauss, was a statehouse employee that Ryan confided in about the photograph and the messages she had seen on the Representative's computer. Ryan had at first been reluctant to give House Counsel Trabucco's name but eventually agreed when assured by Attorneys Kennedy and Fleming that Trabucco would not be in any trouble.

Kennedy started the interview with a request addressed to Trabucco about confidentiality.

"I want to ask you to keep our conversation confidential. I have already talked to the Chairman and told him that I needed to speak to you and that you are not in any kind of trouble."

Kennedy continued, "The only reason you are part of the investigation is that we think you may have information regarding an employee complaint. If you have information, that's fine, and if you don't have any information, that's fine too."

Kennedy added, "Again, I want to stress that you are not in trouble and have done nothing wrong."

Trabucco acknowledged Kennedy's comments.

"First, do you work for Chairman Strauss?"

"Yes, I am the Chief of Staff to Chairman Strauss. I've worked for him for almost 10 years."

Kennedy and Trabucco had a brief conversation about Beth, the Chairman's previous Chief of Staff.

"Do you know Jamie (Ryan)?"

"Just from the building. We're smoking pals – or at least we were, I just quit. I never worked in the same office or suite. I just met her outside, girl talk, that's all."

"Do you know who Jamie works for?"

"Yes, she works for Representative Fresolo."

"Are you aware of any issues that Jamie had with Representative Fresolo?"

"Yes."

"What were those issues?"

"Jamie came to my confidentially asking if I knew of any jobs in the building. That was in December (2012), maybe. I said I did not. She thought maybe we had one. I said I'd keep my eyes open. I asked, everything okay? She said no. I told her to go to HR (Human Resources). Then she started to cry.

"She said her boss was doing things he's not supposed to be doing on his computer. I didn't think she was going to tell me, but then she did. I wish she hadn't told me. I wish I didn't know."

Trabucco continued, "I told her – you need to go downstairs. She went downstairs, and they told her to come back in a few months when there might be an opening. I don't know who she talked to."

Continuing, Trabucco said, "They told her to wait until February when the building starts to move around. I did say to her, I wouldn't mention anything about the picture when she went to HR. I said you shouldn't get into that picture. It was the end of November, early December when I spoke to her."

Trabucco continued, "She told me she went to HR. She said that things weren't working out. She thought it best she should transfer to another office. They said to wait until February. We never talked about it after that."

"What exactly had Jamie told you?"

"Jamie told me that her boss sent a picture of his penis from the State House computer. She said he didn't send it to her. She also said that when she was checking his Facebook account – she updates it for him, I don't do Facebook for my boss – when she was updating it, an IM (Instant Message) came in, and the girl said something to the effect that she liked when the Rep licked her pussy."

Trabucco added, "Jamie told me about the Facebook issue recently, approximately two weeks ago. She asked me if we could talk again. She asked if there was a room we could talk privately. She came in. She said – I need to get out of there. That's when she told me about the Facebook message."

Trabucco continued that she met with Jamie two weeks ago.

"Jamie told me that she was not waiting to get a transfer. She felt she shouldn't have to come to work and see those things. He sent her a text while we were talking, and Jamie said – Now he's telling me I have to do campaign stuff in the building."

"I said to her I don't want to know. I said we can't talk about this stuff."

Kennedy probed for Trabucco to recall the exact date when she last spoke to Jamie.

"I think it might have been last Thursday, March 7. She told me she was going on paid administrative leave. She said I want to thank you for listening to me. She asked me if I told anybody. I told her I had not."

Trabucco continued, "I'm ashamed that I even know this information. Jamie thanked me for being a friend to her."

Kennedy asked, "Have you had any further contact with Jamie?"

"Jamie sent me an email through Facebook to see if I had heard anything. She asked if anyone in the building was talking about it?"

"I told her no. I know she was in the building on Wednesday. I asked her what she was doing here, and she said she had to come in here and talk to House Counsel. I asked if they had found her a job, and she said no."

Trabucco added, "Jamie said she told House Counsel that she had told me about the picture. I said okay, fine, and that was it. Jamie then asked, would I mind if they called me? I said that was fine, but I was mad at her. I prefer that she didn't bring me into it."

Kennedy and Fleming offered an explanation about Jamie naming Trabucco.

"We asked Jamie for this information and Jamie had been very reluctant to disclose your name. We explained to her that it was important that we speak with all the witnesses who had information about this matter, which is why we asked Jamie for your name."

"It was good to know that, and I appreciate knowing that."

"Cindy, are you aware of any other complaints?"

"I saw a text he sent her. She went to get lunch. It might have been the summer before she got married. She told me that she went to get a salad and that she didn't have her cell. She called him back. She said she was gone for 17 minutes. He said I don't give a shit where you were."

Trabucco continued, "There was a text, something about an aide in the district office who supposedly does the Reps campaign work, but the Rep wanted her to do stuff for a political campaign."

"Was Jamie complaining about being asked to do campaign work?"

"No, Jamie was not complaining."

"I didn't mean to use the word complaining. That was a poor choice of words. I meant to ask, was Jamie describing the campaign work?"

"That's right. She was just describing what the Rep was asking her to do. She was saying, you know – I'm not supposed to be doing this stuff here either. He told her you will do it, or I'll find somebody who will. He said he has an aide in the district who does it."

"What, if anything did you say in response to Jamie?"

"I said you need to get out of that office. You're going to get in trouble."

"Did Jamie mention anything else about the district aide?"

"She told me she had only met him once. I was flattered that Jamie confided in me."

"Was there anything else that you think we should know about your conversations with Jamie?"

"I think you ought to know the girl was pretty upset. She was shaking and crying in the Chairman's office two weeks ago when she described the Facebook thing. I wish that HR had just transferred Jamie back in December. I was holding her hand and trying to calm her down."

Trabucco stated that Jamie said, "I didn't ask for this."

"I said, I can't see a girl coming in and having to see that sort of thing. I wish they had given her a job then, when she first went down to HR, but they never moved her."

"Well, Cindy, you gave Jamie very good advice about going down to HR. That was good. You did the right thing."

"I honestly, I actually have been praying for her. I didn't see the picture, but I just thought of this girl coming to work and having to see this. It's wrong. I did not see the picture. I did not see anything. But I do think it's wrong."

(Trabucco was emotional at this point and began to tear up.)

"I want to thank you for coming in, and I want to remind you about the importance of keeping the conversation confidential."

"You have no worries on that front. I never told anybody, and I don't want to tell anybody. I told Jamie she needed to be careful. I told her, the way this place works, it's gonna come back on you."

"Jamie is not in trouble, and neither are you. Again, thanks for your time."

Friday, March 15, 2013

Annie Martin-McDonough, a former aide to Fresolo, became a target for an interview as Ryan mentioned her has having claimed that Fresolo asked her to lie for him. She apparently took the job as Fresolo's aide reluctantly and was relieved when within six weeks of starting in Fresolo's office she was offered a chance to move to a different job in the State House.

Kennedy opened the interview with Annie Martin-McDonough with an admonishment against discussing the conversation with anyone.

"This is a confidential meeting. Please don't discuss this conversation with anyone. Not with the Chairman who you now work for or his Chief of Staff. If they ask, please tell them I directed you not to discuss it. I spoke to the Chairman, and he's aware of this meeting. I don't expect that he or the Chief of Staff will ask you about this."

Kennedy continued, "You haven't done anything wrong. I'm sure it's a little intimidating coming down here and being told that your name has come up in an investigation, but I promise to make it as painless as possible."

"First, can you just tell us about your employment history?"

"Well, I was an intern for a former Rep. Then I worked for her for two years as an aide. When my former employer left the House in 2011, I worked for Representative Fresolo for two months. My time with my former Rep was from May 2010 until January 2011, an election year. I worked for Fresolo for two months in early 2011."

Martin-McDonough continued, "I am now working for a third Rep where I have been for the last two years."

"Can you tell us about your time with Representative Fresolo?"

"I didn't want to take the job. He has a less than great reputation in the building. As soon as I started, I pretty much didn't want to be there. The Chairman moved in, and luckily, I was able to get a position with him."

"I know it's difficult to have a conversation about members. It's not going to get you in trouble, but please feel free, to be honest, and candid with us about what it was like to work with Representative Fresolo."

"Well, during the interview, in the middle of the interview, he said – if you Google me, really terrible things come up, are you okay with that? He also asked - will you run against me? So, that's how things started."

Martin-McDonough continued, "There was an extra paycheck (paystub) that I had to leave on his desk every two weeks, and he told me not to ask any questions. That's probably the best answer I can give about what it was like to work for Representative Fresolo. I left an extra paycheck stub on the corner every two weeks and was told not to ask questions."

Martin-McDonough added, "He had a less than stellar reputation. Politically I didn't agree with him. He's received bad press in the past for not being upstanding. I never wanted to work for him. I consider it a black stain on my career that I ever did work for him."

"The Speaker's Office has asked me to investigate certain matters related to Representative Fresolo. Do you remember anything else about working for him, and please do not hold back?"

"The truth is I didn't ask about the other paycheck. But I was instructed not to ask."

"Were there any other issues during those two months?"

"The Rep files a number of per diems for transportation. I knew he wasn't coming in every day. I just let that happen. Janet Wu (TV Reporter) was doing a story, he asked me to lie to her and say that his daughter had been in a car accident. I told him that he couldn't make me do that; that I wouldn't do that. The day after he asked me to do that, I quit."

Martin-McDonough continued, "I was uncomfortable writing so many recommendation letters for the same five people who were unqualified for the positions they were seeking. These were his friends in Worcester. One of them was a person by the last name of Rocco. I have those files. I have files from when I worked for him because I use them as templates as letter writing."

"Please send us those files."

"Okay."

Martin-McDonough made a point about what he asked her to do.

"Representative Fresolo never instructed me to do anything that was outright illegal."

"Other than the per diem and the Janet Wu interview, did he ever instruct you to do anything else that made you uncomfortable?"

"I didn't like doing favors for the same couple people in Worcester over and over again."

Kennedy asked about access to his email.

"The Rep gave me access to his email. I did review those. But just made basic replies like thank you for your opinion."

"Did you ever see anything on the email system that was of concern to you?"

"I apologize, I wish I remembered. There were little things. Those things that led me to quit my job. I'm sorry, I wish I remembered better."

"What can you tell me about his Facebook page?"

"I don't remember having access to the Rep's Facebook. He has his own account. He didn't use his personal Facebook page."

"Did he ever ask you to help with his campaign?"

"I sensed it was heading in that direction, which is why I wanted out as quickly as I did it. I discovered that there were templates for campaign type things that I inherited from the prior aide. Like a little card – I'm holding a fundraiser."

Martin-McDonough added, "The Rep I work for now does that type of work from his house. I saw them in the State House when I worked for Representative Fresolo, and I thought that's probably not legal. I told myself I'm not going to do that if he asks. I never called the ethics commission to ask if it was legal or not, but from ethics training in the building, I knew it wasn't right."

Fleming spoke up, "Annie, what kind of – favors – was the Representative performing for the same people in Worcester?"

"They were job recommendations; turnpike jobs, toll-taking jobs.

Kennedy asked, "Have you had any contact with the Representative's family?"

"I met his daughter, the younger one when he was re-elected. That was it. His family members didn't call."

Martin-McDonough added, "There was a police officer in Worcester who got prosecuted for attacking a person. He was a frequent caller. He wanted a job with the DOC (Department of Corrections)."

"Annie, can you confirm for me that the Representative only attended formal sessions while you worked for him?"

"Yes, he came in for formal sessions. After I moved to work for the Chairman, we were still in the same office suite. I think he may have attended hearings, but I don't know."

"Do you know Jamie Ryan?"

"Yes, I know his current aide."

"Has Jamie mentioned anything to you about Representative Fresolo?"

"I feel bad for Jamie. He picked up with her where he left off with me. While I got to ignore who Ken was, Jamie couldn't."

"Why do you think that she couldn't ignore Ken?"

"I don't know why she had to talk to him. I think the fact that they weren't having actual conversations. I believe that Ken doesn't really work for Representative Fresolo, or only in a limited capacity."

"Can you think of anything else that Jamie may have said about her work environment?"

"She convinced him to put his email on his cell phone. He became more responsible for that (using and answering email). He became more active on Facebook. He used it as a dating website, and Jamie had to read all kinds of inappropriate things."

"Do you know why Jamie suggested he get a smartphone and put his emails on his phone?"

"Because she wanted him to be a part of the 21st Century. It's easier to communicate that way. I think she was like; this is what a smartphone is. She had access to his email, just like I did."

Martin-McDonough confirmed that in addition to having access to the Representative's email, she changed his password.

"I don't know if he knew how to change his password; presumably, he did, but I'm not sure. When I worked for him, he accessed his email from home. He didn't have a smartphone at that time. At some point, you couldn't update your password from remote access through Outlook. He's in almost constant communication with his aide. He would call in response to emails."

"How many times a day would he call?"

"It was not unusual for the Rep to call me 10 times a day. I think he was nicer to me than he is to Jamie. I think that may be because Jamie comes across as a tougher person than I am."

"Did Jamie indicate to you that she had his Facebook password?"

"She must have had his password because she could see all his info. There were messages from random women."

"Did she describe those messages?"

"Yes, they were sometimes explicit in nature. She told me this a couple months ago. They moved to another office, so I stopped seeing Jamie as much. I don't know what they are doing now, which is a relief."

"Anything else we should know?"

"I don't remember all of the little things. I can't really be helpful. I'm sorry."

Fleming interjected, "Did the Representative ever sexually harass you?"

"No, he didn't. Sometimes he would bring people into the office who would say inappropriate things."

Martin-McDonough mentioned former Representative Johnny Rucho and joked that he was probably 100 years old.

"He would say really sexist and inappropriate things. The aide before me was Paul McGlory, so it had been an all-male environment, so I think it took some getting used to."

"Do you remember any of the comments he made?"

"They were just overt sexual misogynistic comments. I was in the office with him. I could hear it and just ignored it.

He would bring in Timmy as well. Timmy works for another member. Timmy was lifelong friends with Representative Fresolo. He has a learning disability. He doesn't work here. Not a paid staffer. He would come in every time that Representative Fresolo came in. There was a split when Representative Fresolo considered running for the Senate, and now he comes in with another member."

"Did you ever witness him sexually harass anyone else?"

"No, but everything about working for him made me uncomfortable. Obviously working there was not what I wanted since I was there only two months. I'd rather not associate myself with him."

Martin-McDonough went on to explain when she left working for Fresolo.

"When I told the Rep, I was quitting he swallowed and asked why. He left and came back, and he said, "okay." I don't feel bad now. When he hired me, he said I need a year commitment from you. But I just couldn't stay."

Martin-McDonough explained that she continued to work in the same office as Representative Fresolo for more than a year, but they never spoke again.

"He's not there very often."

Fleming asked, "Did you Google him at any point?"

"Yes, I found the stories about him from before. These were all the things that people knew in the building, which is part of why it was so hard to take the job."

"Did you ever talk with anyone else in the building about Representative Fresolo?"

"Yes, I talked to the member I formerly worked for and the member I currently work for. I spoke to the former member, and she said - don't do what he asks; you need to get out of there. Thank God, it was good grace, the Chairman offered me a job. I never had to leave the building. My intent was that I was going to quit even though I didn't have a job. It was the day after he didn't take the interview with Janet Wu. I quit, and the Chairman just happened to pick me up the next day."

Kennedy wanted to get more detail about her quitting.

"Please give me some detail on why and how you quit?"

"Janet Wu was doing a story on per diems and campaign fundraisers. It wasn't so much lying to Janet Wu. It was that, since he asked me to lie, you can't really deny that there is something to lie about. I just figured there would be no going back."

"Did you speak to anyone else about why you quit?"

"I spoke to my friend Danielle who was on the committee staff in public service. Just a casual friend. I never had any interaction with HR. I didn't know what to do. I was out there and kept my head down. I hope my short duration is a sign of my good faith in not wanting to be involved in it."

Martin-McDonough continued, "Jamie is a talkative person. I assume that this is how it came up."

Kennedy denied that Jamie is the origin of the complaint. He thanked her for coming in. The Interview concluded.

Friday, March 15, 2013

James M. Murphy, Representative for the 4th Norfolk District, was a former supervisor of Jamie Ryan. She left her job with Murphy to take a position in private industry mostly for the increased pay. However, she decided to come back to the State House when she became disillusioned with the private sector job. That's when she took the position as administrative aide to Representative Fresolo.

Kennedy contacted Murphy by telephone.

"I want to inform you that this is an employee matter, an HR matter. The Speaker has asked me to look into it. Your name came up. We ask that you keep this conversation strictly confidential. Your name came up as someone who might have information, or you may not. Either way, hopefully, we will never have to discuss this again."

"I understand."

"Do you know Jamie Ryan?"

"Yes, Jamie worked for me a few years ago. I'm not sure of the exact dates. She was two aides ago for me, so maybe two to three years ago. She worked for me for a year or two. Somewhere around there."

"What can you remember about her departure?"

"Jamie worked for me, and she left to take a sales job outside the building. She left, I'm not sure what she was selling."

"How would you describe that departure?"

"It was friendly."

"Did she have any issues or concerns?"

"Nothing out of the ordinary that I can remember."

"Have you spoken with her since?"

"I see her around the building. I say hello to her. Pleasant short conversations. I couldn't tell you the last time we talked, but we do say hi."

"Do you know where she works now?"

"She works for John Fresolo."

"When you've seen her, has she mentioned anything about her current position; did she ever raise any concerns?"

"Never, no. When she left me and started working for John, we never had any conversation about John. It's more like hey, how you doing? We don't have work conversations. We are still friendly. I say hi to her. I knew her because her mother manages an Irish radio station. She asked me to look at her daughter. I took her resume, she looked like a good candidate."

"Anything else that might be helpful to us?"

"I've always had a good relationship with her. She was a good worker for me." The interview concluded.

Part Two – Kangaroo Court

kan-ga-roo court

noun

- an unofficial court held by a group of people in order to try someone regarded, especially without good evidence, as guilty of a crime or misdemeanor.

Richard F. Wright

Chapter Four

Executive Conference

Friday, March 15, 2013

The letter to Martin J. Walsh, Chairman of the House Committee on Ethics, was dated March 15, 2012, and was signed by Speaker of the House Robert DeLeo. The letter directed Chairman Walsh to begin an investigation and evaluation of the alleged violations of Rule 16A by Representative John Fresolo. Enclosed with the letter was a copy of the preliminary report upon which the Speaker had made the decision to proceed. Chairman Walsh was about to embark on a professional and political journey he could never have previously imagined. A fellow Representative, a colleague, a friend, was under attack for alleged violations of the ethical rules of the House and it fell to him to set up the investigation, determine how to proceed, schedule everyone involved to testify and many other things he hadn't yet imagined.

Walsh was a legislator, a lawmaker, and in the State House environment, he reacted the same way John Fresolo had reacted when laws and rules were concerned. Both men realized they needed a lawyer. Fresolo picked Thomas Kiley on the recommendation of a friend. Walsh and the committee finally secured the services of Thomas Frongillo, of the law firm *Fish and Richardson* in Boston.

Under House Rules, the committee had several ways to proceed with its investigation. Chairman Walsh elected to use the Executive Conference procedure as it provided, in essence, that the entire process would be confidential. No posting of sessions was required, no transcription or recording of the proceedings was required, and whoever was the target of the investigation would be allowed to have counsel, as long as his attorney did not participate in the proceedings.

Walsh spent a lot of time preparing for the Executive Conference. He consulted with the Office of Legal Counsel and with his newly appointed legal counsel, Frongillo. It would become necessary for subpoenas to be sent out so that the committee could control the time and location of the Executive Conference sessions.

As the term Executive Conference was obscure in usage, the proceedings were variously described by committee members, the media, and the public as "hearings." Typically, a hearing is public, certain protective rules apply to ensure fairness, and there are various appeal processes available. But, in the format of an Executive Conference under the Massachusetts House Rules 16A the procedure is "secret." To date, none of the preliminary or final reports have been officially released to the public.

Circa Thursday, March 21, 2013

On or about Thursday, March 21, the Speaker asked two Representatives their opinion and advice. It may be instructive to understand something about these two men. Some background:

It's an accepted fact that nothing moves faster in time and space than political news. It can be real news or junk news, but it always moves fast. Vincent Pedone (D-Worcester) was a 10-term Representative for the 15th Worcester District, which was adjacent to Fresolo's 16th District. When Fresolo was first elected to his seat, vacated by Guy Glodis who successfully ran for Senator in the 2nd Worcester District in 2000, he became acquainted with Representative John Binienda with whom he became great friends. Binienda had known Glodis for a long time before he ran and won the election in the 16th.

For reasons that have never been clear, Glodis and Binienda jointly suggested to Fresolo that when redistricting came up that year, he should petition to get the notably "Italo" (5-3) precinct back into his district that Bill Glodis (Guy's Dad) surrendered to Representative Andy Collaro many years ago.

Naively, Fresolo marched down and made the request. As soon as he did, Glodis and Binienda tattled to Pedone that Fresolo was trying to take one of his precincts.

Pedone lost his mind. He confronted Fresolo, who did not deny that he had made the request, but he honestly didn't understand the hornet's nest he'd stirred up.

Pedone said, "Let me tell you something. That's my fuckin' district, and redistricting is based on seniority; I'll fuck you over, don't you ever think I won't."

Fresolo was aghast at the outburst. He finally got a word in edgewise and told Pedone it was Glodis and Binienda that suggested he make a move.

Fresolo said, "Didn't Glodis give the precinct to Collaro 10 years ago?"

Pedone acknowledged that he did.

"Well, then how would I know anything about this unless Guy and John told me? They tell me to go and make a move and then they go and tell you I'm making a move. How sick is that?"

Now, well off on the wrong foot, Pedone and Fresolo remained unfriendly to each other to this day.

At some point when the Speaker got further updates on the on-going investigation, he picked up the phone and called Binienda and Pedone. He may have called others too. He asked them what they thought and what he should do?

Fresolo later heard from insiders that both of them green-lighted the full investigation of Fresolo. Neither sought to quiet it down for Fresolo's sake. Pedone didn't like Fresolo and Binienda had a recent falling out with Fresolo and found this an opportunity to be cruel to his former friend, without having a direct hand in the play.

The next move was pure Pedone: he called Jordan Levy, the Worcester radio talk-show host to tell him that Fresolo was on the hot seat. He spiced it up by claiming Fresolo would be gone in 48 hours. He also tipped off Walter Bird, at the *Worcester Magazine*, who put an update on its website. That played perfectly into bamboozling Jordan Levy, as he had a well-known journalistic policy not to report spicy-bits unless he had two sources. He proudly announced on his show that Fresolo would "resign within the next 48 hours."

The two sources, in this case, were (1) Vinny Pedone, via Jordan Levy direct, and (2) Vinny Pedone, via Walter Bird, indirect through *Worcester Magazine*.

Friday, March 22, 2013

Matt Murphy and Andy Metzer of the *State House News Service* in Boston released a story that House Speaker Robert DeLeo had opened an investigation into serious allegations against an unnamed member of the House of Representatives.

The reporters wrote that Jim Kennedy, of the Office of Legal Counsel, had brought the allegations forward earlier and that the Speaker had ordered an investigation.

Tying the statement from DeLeo's spokesperson, Seth Gitell, to comments the previous night by the Worcester radio talk-show host, Jordan Levy, that Fresolo would resign in the next 48 hours, the cat seemed out of the bag. The "secret" proceedings were now front-page headlines, talk-show fodder, and it brought the TV cameras of Janet Wu from WCVB-TV in Boston onto Fresolo's driveway in Worcester.

Janet Wu confronted Fresolo as he entered his driveway and then proceeded to follow him into his garage. She continued to ask questions while he continuously refused to answer the questions from her ambush interview. On television that night, Wu used videotape of her pursuit up the driveway that day at Fresolo's house and tape from two years ago when she was following up on the per diem reports that local media post every two years about legislators being compensated for commuting to work.

In her earlier interview, she asks if John came to work all of the days he claimed, and he answered, "I do not apologize for going to work." The interview she taped for Channel 5 two years earlier was never shown at the time, although it was posted on its website. But now, it echoed nicely with her ambush questions today about whether he was the subject of the now public investigation of an "unnamed" legislator.

The *Worcester Telegram* had a reporter call who asked Fresolo if he was resigning. John told him no and ended the call. So much for a confidential investigation by the ethics committee.

Sunday, March 24, 2013

After the news of the investigation was released by House Leadership, Dianne Williamson, a columnist for the *Worcester Telegram*, wrote a story where she cited the headlines and commentary that had appeared in the *Worcester Magazine* and on the WTAG radio talk-show hosted by Jordan Levy. She also commented on the well-known Boston blogger, Michele McPhee, all of whom had the story that Fresolo had been naughty. She went on to point out that the "story was dubbed so salacious" that it had appeared in the *Daily Mail* in London, England.

Other coverage of the unfolding story was provided by various online news organizations including the *Boston Herald*, the *Boston Globe*, *InCityTimes*, *MassLive*, the *Sentinel and Enterprise*, *CBS Boston*, and *examiner.com*. Each had the same general details of the investigation underway of an "unnamed" individual, but each in turn named Fresolo as the subject, apparently happy to give attribution to other media outlets. It was a happy, cooperative feeding frenzy.

The only unique aspect of the story was the way each dipped into the euphemism bag and came up with various headlines:

- Rep *Sends Dirty Pix* To Female Co-worker
- The Anthony Weiner of Worcester
- Fresolo Under Investigation For *Explicit* Photos
- State Rep *Sent Pictures* Of His Genitals via Government Computer
- Mass Legislator in Hot Water Over *Dirty Pics*

The *italic* emphasis is mine to point out the publications were delighted to claim Fresolo *deliberately* sent the pictures to a specific person – who it would be implied did not seek to see the pictures, or expected to see the pictures - therefore could be interpreted as harassing behavior.

The reporting stopped at the gate of secrecy imposed by the investigation process that Chairman Walsh had elected to use. An Executive Conference is intended to be confidential and neither the Speaker, the Chairman, or for that matter, the accused may comment; otherwise they are in violation of the House Rules guiding the process.

A suspicious person might detect that using the cover of an "unnamed" target allowed the State to release a statement about an investigation and let the media take the bait and go ahead and "name" someone: Fresolo, while House Leadership stayed within the rules of confidentiality.

Fresolo had to scurry away from ambush media to avoid being in further hot water with the House Leadership and had no cover from the bad look it presented to the public.

Monday, March 25, 2013

Representative Jason Lewis took it upon himself to reach out to the Office of Legal Counsel and offered to be interviewed on his direct knowledge of the situation. He had read and seen the reports of the investigation along with everyone else in the State House over the past week. On Monday, March 25, 2013, Representative Jason Lewis (31st Middlesex District), who shares general office space with Representative Fresolo's office, approached House Counsel and asked to meet to discuss the allegations that had been made against Fresolo.

On Tuesday, March 26, 2013, Representative Lewis came to a meeting that started at 4:45 PM to discuss things he either had personal knowledge or had secondhand knowledge of, through his aide, who sat close to Ryan.

Kennedy thanked the Representative for contacting him and asked him to proceed with what he wanted to tell them.

"I saw in the (Boston) *Herald* the number of days that Representative Fresolo has put in for per diems. It is a lot if I see Representative Fresolo in the building once a week. I have personally observed Representative Fresolo in the building for full formal sessions and not much else."

Lewis continued, "I'm usually in the building Tuesday through Thursday. I occasionally see Representative Fresolo here on Wednesdays when the House has a full formal session. Other than those days when the House has a full formal session, I can count on one hand the number of times I have seen the Representative in the building."

"When I saw the *Herald* report that Representative Fresolo had put in for 200 plus days, it was just inconceivable to me. That would be a little over four days a week. This is just inconceivable to me that he would put in for so many days."

Lewis pointed out that he worked near Representative Fresolo's office for approximately 18 months and that they overlapped for the entire calendar year of 2012.

"I never thought too much of the fact that Representative Fresolo wasn't in the office much. If I lived out in Worcester, I wouldn't come in that much either. But I could not imagine how Representative Fresolo could claim to be here 200 days a year."

Kennedy asked Representative Lewis if he was on any of the same committees as Representative Fresolo?

"No, I am not, so I would not know if he was here for committee meetings. But again, it is extremely rare to see him in the building other than when the House has a formal session."

Lewis now turned his comments to the allegation about Fresolo's district aide.

"My legislative aide has worked for me for three years, and I have never questioned anything she has ever done. I trust her to be honest and believe that she has impeccable judgment. I'm aware of this next item through my aide.

"I understand that Representative Fresolo has a paid aide that he has had for some time. This pre-dates Jamie Ryan and was true even under Representative Fresolo's previous aide, Paul McClory."

Lewis stated that his legislative aide had seen a paycheck for (Fresolo's) district aide. He continued.

"My aide talked to Jamie Ryan and said that Ryan had never worked with the district aide on any constituent matter or any policy work."

"When Jamie was on her honeymoon, she had to get another aide, Alicia Spadafore, to fill in for her while she was gone. This didn't make any sense to me; why would Jamie need to get another aide to fill in for her while she was away if Representative Fresolo already had a district aide? My aide told me that the only thing the district aide seemed to work on was fundraising."

Lewis pointed out that his aide had brought this situation to his attention before these allegations against Fresolo came to light.

"My aide told me Jamie had never met Representative Fresolo's district aide or worked with him on anything. I asked my aide whether he had a district office, thinking perhaps the person was staffing a district office and handling walk-ins. My aide told me there was no district office and that he worked out of his home. I didn't question it because I didn't think it was my business, but that it did seem a little odd."

Lewis brought up another allegation with which he had some information.

"My aide was called over by Jamie to her computer one day when the Representative was out. I was not in the office when this occurred, but my aide had relayed the following information to me. Jamie had been on her honeymoon. When she came back, she was going through the Representative's email to catch up on constituent work. Apparently, she clicked on this attachment and had a very unpleasant experience. She was surprised and called my aide over just to say, this happened, and my aide saw it and had a very unpleasant experience."

Lewis continued, "My aide told me about this the next time I was in the State House. It would have been whenever Jamie got back from her honeymoon. My aide came to talk to me about it and said this is really gross. I had known about this for a while before any of these allegations came to light.

Lewis next brought up an allegation about employment recommendations.

"I know everyone is struggling with how to make employment recommendations in light of the new advisory. I am fortunate that in my district I don't get many requests, but Jamie would tell my aide that she spent almost all her time trying to find jobs for people the Representative knew including relatives like his nephew. Jamie seemed unhappy about it according to my aide. Jamie was under a lot of pressure to do whatever she could to find those people jobs in state government. My aide said Jamie was asked to make calls, to follow-up."

Lewis pointed out that he talked about these issues, and the pressure Jamie was under with his aide around the time the advisory came out, which was several weeks before any allegations against Representative Fresolo became public.

"My aide told me that Jamie said Fresolo would have her do fundraising work in the State House or on her work computer. Jamie knew she wasn't supposed to do it, but that the Representative told her that she had to do it. Jamie was very conflicted. I don't know exactly what campaign work Jamie was asked to perform, but I know it included invitations to fundraisers. Jamie felt these were things she had to do."

Lewis stated that these were the allegations he was aware of and that he felt compelled to come forward.

"If Jamie had put her employment at risk to address these issues, I felt it was important that I share whatever information I had about all this with House Counsel."

Kennedy thanked the Representative for coming, and the meeting concluded.

Tuesday, March 26, 2013

Ken Simoncini, a longtime friend, and district aide to Representative Fresolo was fired today. He received a letter terminating him effective the previous March 20, 2013, specifying his contradictory statements about how many hours he worked per week for John Fresolo. When given a chance to make a formal statement in the form of an affidavit, he wrote that he averaged between "18 to 20" hours of work per week. His termination letter indicated he was being released for cause. They rejected his sworn affirmation as false because it directly contradicted statements he had made during the visit he made to the Counsel's office on March 15, 2013.

Fresolo had mixed feelings about Simoncini's situation. At the meeting where House Counsel asked a lot of questions, he had not been sworn in as he would expect at a deposition, and he had not been allowed to know the nature and intent of the questioning ahead of time that would take place at that interview. He had no legal counsel and no time to prepare his answers. So, his somewhat casual and slightly combative demeanor, which Fresolo was familiar with, had led him to give a misleading description of his work schedule. There was nothing Fresolo could do to help him.

But, for Kennedy, it was a convenient way to release someone who was an employee at will in the Commonwealth. Under Massachusetts law, unless protected by contract terms or union affiliation, anyone can be fired without any reason given at all. Although the law requires that he be paid any owed wages on the day of release, Kennedy didn't bother with that.

Thursday, April 4, 2013

On or about April 4, 2013, the House Committee on Rules, in response to a request received from Chairman Walsh, agreed to authorize subpoena power to the House Committee on Ethics. The Rules Committee was chaired, ironically, by Binienda, the longtime friend, colleague, and ride-sharer, with Fresolo. Ultimately, Binienda was subject to one of the subpoena's he authorized.

The Witness list created by the committee had 42 names on it, to begin with. Eventually, some of those on the list were dropped, and others were added. Not all witnesses that received a subpoena actually were called to testify.

Friday, April 5, 2013

On Friday, April 5, 2013, Chairman Walsh sent by hand and certified-mail a letter to John Fresolo advising him that a complaint had been received by the Committee on Ethics, pursuant to House Rule 16. The letter referenced an enclosed document that enumerated 13 allegations, it provided a list of witnesses that may be summoned, it advised he could bring an attorney, and it identified the date of the Executive Conference on Tuesday, April 9, 2013, at 1:30 PM in Room 348 of the Massachusetts State House.

Shockingly, instead of the original seven allegations, the communication listed 13 allegations. The Office of Legal Counsel had generated six more allegations attributed to Jamie Ryan. She had apparently given it some more thought to determine if there were other things Fresolo had been doing wrong.

The fast-evolving situation around the investigation of Fresolo gave Walsh a chance to reconsider the benefits of being a committee Chairman. It had been well known in the

House that as a member of this committee you would not meet very often and when you did it would be to roll over some updates to the adopted ethics rules of the House. It was an opportunity not unfamiliar to other friends of House Leadership to gather some extra pay without too much heavy lifting. His previous committee assignments, which did not include being a Chairman, were light duty. There had been some rumbling among House members when Walsh got the nod from Speaker DeLeo to become Chairman as he had not been a supporter of DeLeo for Speaker. Walsh, like Fresolo, had supported Representative John Rogers. But, Walsh's strong union credentials were enough to persuade the Speaker to overrule the criticism from his own loyalists.

Now, the possible downside to being Chairman exposed itself. This was going to be time-consuming and fraught with potential political landmines. This was not a welcome situation right now, as Walsh was eyeing a run for Mayor of Boston, and the last thing he needed was an active sub-committee to take up valuable campaign time.

Quickly reviewing his memory on the ethics committee's history, Walsh couldn't even remember a time when a hearing had been held to determine if a fellow house member had committed a breach of ethics that rose to the level of calling for a hearing. He had no guidelines or precedents to turn to on how to proceed. So, he determined he would just have to take the plunge and schedule an Executive Conference and bring the committee together to set up a process to review the allegations against Fresolo.

It was well known in the State House, in Fresolo's District, and among the general public that Fresolo was no friend of the Speaker. He may be a registered Democrat, but his District was a very conservative Democratic district. Abortion, gun control, and the death penalty were trigger points for the Democratically-controlled State House. Fresolo often fell on the wrong side of those issues as seen by the more liberal Democrats in the House.

In Walsh's mind, regardless of the facts uncovered at the upcoming hearing, he was going to be left in the middle between his colleague of long-standing, Fresolo, and the man upstairs, Speaker DeLeo, who controlled his, and everyone else's political destiny. Maybe taking the chairmanship of the light-duty ethics committee had been a mistake? Walsh cleared his head and turned to the matter at hand.

Tuesday, April 9, 2013

Representative Fresolo and his Attorney, Tom Kiley, arrived at Room 348 in the Representative's Lounge area of the State House a few minutes before 1:00 PM. As they entered the room, they realized no one else was there yet. The two stood toward the back of the room to wait and see what the protocol would be. In the middle of the room was a very large conference table with what appeared to be a dozen seats.

It was now early afternoon as the members of the committee filed into Room 348 at the State House. They had obviously assembled somewhere else and came to the room as a group. The 11 committee members took a seat around the oversize conference table. Each committee member had walked in carrying a large white binder filled with tabbed sections that contained letters, reports, and attachments concerning the allegations that had been lodged, the communications from the Speaker on his requirements, and other documents.

The Committee on Ethics consisted of seven members appointed by the Speaker and four who were appointed by the Minority Leader. The composition of the committee included seven men and four women. The Chairman was Martin J. Walsh, D-Dorchester, 13th Suffolk District.

The other members were: Jay **Barrows**, R-Mansfield, 1st Bristol District; Matthew **Beaton**, R-Shrewsbury, 11th Worcester District; Paul **Donato**, D-Medford, 35th Middlesex District; Patricia **Haddad**, D-Somerset, 5th Bristol District; Peter **Kocot**, D-Northampton, 1st Hampshire District; David **Nangle**, D-Lowell, 17th Middlesex District; Shaunna **O'Connell**, D-Taunton, 3rd Bristol District; Elizabeth **Poirier**, R-North Attleborough, 14 Bristol District; Kathi-Anne **Reinstein**, D-Revere, 16th Suffolk District; and Theodore **Spiliotis**, D-Danvers, 13th Essex District.

Fresolo and his Attorney continued to stand and were not invited to sit down. Each stood along the wall along the side of the table. Half of the committee members were seated with their backs to Kiley and Fresolo. Throughout the meeting, those with their backs to them did not turn around to address them or to look at them.

Walsh spoke, "If I may have everyone's attention. This Executive Conference of the House Ethics Committee is called to order. We all know each other, and so we can dispense with introductions. I would point out that Attorney Thomas Frongillo has been engaged to represent the committee and will participate in the hearing on its behalf. Mr. Thomas Kiley appears today as private counsel to Representative John Fresolo, the subject of this hearing," said Walsh.

"First, let me say we will take as long as it takes to complete this investigation. You all need to set your schedules to make sure you are available," said Walsh.

Walsh proceeded to have Attorney Frongillo read out the allegations that had comprised the body of the complaint. He read each one of the 13 items that Fresolo's aide had brought to the attention of the Office of Legal Counsel.

Walsh then recognized Attorney Kiley.

Kiley said, "I want to advise the committee on behalf of Representative Fresolo that we are prepared to cooperate in the inquiry that you are conducting and that we feel once all the pertinent facts are known, the committee will see clear to exonerate John from the many misleading and false allegations that have been lodged against him and therefore adopt a fair judgment on the issues.

As to the process that you plan to follow, I would respectfully request that you consider adopting procedures recommended in instances such as this by the National Conference of State Legislatures for an investigative process that incorporates the right of the accused to present evidence, witnesses, and to cross-examine that which is presented by State on its behalf. Those of you who know me well will remember that when I represented Kevin Fitzgerald in his case, the committee agreed to adopt those guidelines."

Walsh spoke up, "Okay, Mr. Kiley, we will keep that in mind and let you know how we will proceed."

"Before we go further, John, would you like to say something?"

"Yes, Mr. Chairman. First, I can't believe this is happening. These charges don't make any sense. I don't know why she's doing this to me. I've always been good to her; I've gone out of my way to let her have time off when she needed it. I don't understand why she's making these allegations. This girl is a nightmare."

Fresolo's voice cracked, he tried to compose himself. He had been standing along the wall with half of the committee members turned away from him, and the others on the opposite side of the table slumped in their chairs with their heads down, not making eye contact with John.

"I'm sorry for being emotional. I was good to her. You don't understand what it's like to drive up to my house and find Channel 4, 5, and 7 on my lawn. The press is running articles filled with lies and inaccuracies. My family has to see this stuff on TV. I have to try to calm my two daughters. The reporters are stopping people at the supermarket and asking questions about me."

"I've always worked hard for my district. I've never done anything to hurt anybody and for people now to think things because of her making false accusations. It's not right."

Shifting his weight from one foot to the other, John tried to use his voice to command their attention.

"You should know that I did not send that photo to my aide. I did not use the House system for personal messages. I'm looking forward to making my side clear to all of you."

The Committee spent a few more minutes listening to Attorney Frongillo describe the subpoena process, the general scheduling as of now, and how they will be notified when the next session would be set. The entire meeting had lasted no more than 15 minutes. Everyone filed out without acknowledging Fresolo or Kiley and without any comments.

Walking down the corridor together, Fresolo turned to Kiley and said, "That did not go well."

Kiley responded, "I agree. That did not go well."

Wednesday, April 10, 2013

Attorney Tom Kiley went right to work coordinating the collection of the evidence that the ethics committee had, which might be brought forward during the next Executive Conference. As he negotiated back and forth with Attorney Frongillo, who spoke on behalf of the ethics committee, he learned of the process they were following. The committee was actively seeking telephone records, credit card records, highway transponder records, parking pass records, and financial and other background information about John Fresolo.

They were actively engaged in analyzing and comparing the number of pings on the EZ Pass system with the pings on the parking at the State House and in comparison to phone calls made from Fresolo's cell phone. Data was secured that showed when and where he made calls and how they compared to the transportation records. If, for example, Fresolo filed for a per diem on a day where he bought gas in Worcester, talked on the phone from Worcester, and had no EZ Pass ping recorded, it would be easy to claim he had not been in Boston that day. The committee's Attorney was looking for that kind of evidence. Combing through the records was a tedious process, and the law firm of *Fish and*

Richardson put a lot of staff time, and billing, into the process. Attorney Frongillo felt this would be part of the smoking gun evidence that would sink Fresolo.

Attorney Kiley asked Fresolo to come to his office over the next few weeks and pour over these transponder records and compare them to the printouts of his telephone calls. The pile of records was enormous, and the more that he studied the records, the more confusing it got. There were some days when his EZ Pass and parking records showed he was in Boston quite clearly, yet there were phone calls apparently originating from towers in the Worcester area. How was that possible? Fresolo's cell phone was attached to his fist tighter than his own five fingers. No one would be using his phone in Worcester while he was at the State House, so it was alarming to see these contradictory results. Didn't Walsh and the committee see how bad the data was?

Monday, April 15, 2013

Tragically, on the afternoon of the Boston Marathon, at 2:49 PM the city and the country were shattered by two pressure cooker bombs detonated at the finish line of the Marathon, killing three people, maiming and injuring hundreds of more bystanders, including 16 who lost limbs. Along with everyone else with important things to do, Fresolo's personal struggle to prepare a defense against the allegations had to be put on hold, as the city spent a week searching for the bombers and trying to understand what had happened and why.

The Governor closed the city and most of the government employees, except essential personnel, were kept away from the State House. Where people could manage it, they worked from home or from other locations if possible. A lot of the public transportation system was temporarily shut down. Fresolo stayed in touch with his Attorney and tried to keep things in focus. He was anxious to understand how the next step in the hearing process would proceed, but he had to wait to hear from Kiley and from the committee. No hearing date had been set yet.

Monday, April 22, 2013

A certain amount of normalcy returned to the city and the country following the past week's pain and tension surrounding the Marathon bombing. The search for the terrorists, the capture of one and the demise of the second had been exhausting, even for those who stared blindly at the television screen waiting for news bits that came slowly and infrequently, if not at all. The tragedy of the event, the heroism of the first responders, the bewilderment about the perpetrators, and what could they have been thinking, were important stories that filled the headlines. The John Fresolo Saga was back page news for a while. That was soon to change.

Circa April 24, 2013

Attorney Kiley received a message from Attorney Frongillo suggesting that a meeting be set for a status check on the schedule for the next Executive Conference and to exchange information on further evidence that the State had prepared. While privileged work product was not something they would share with Fresolo, they had committed to making available any data or other information they had been collecting in its raw form. How they interpreted it or what they thought was important was not something they would share.

Attorney Thomas C. Frongillo had just joined *Fish and Richardson* in the past month having parted ways with *Weil, Gotshal & Manges*. Frongillo is a former Assistant US Attorney for the District of Massachusetts. The significance of this assignment as Special Counsel to the Committee on Ethics for the Massachusetts House of Representatives can't be underestimated. As of this writing, six years since the case was handled, it's one of two cases listed on the corporate website as indicative of Frongillo's successful career.

His opponent in this fight, Attorney Thomas R. Kiley, is a partner in the law firm, *Cosgrove, Eisenberg & Kiley* of Boston. Kiley is a former Massachusetts Assistant Attorney General. Kiley was also a veteran of the Vietnam war where his tour ended abruptly with his left side partially paralyzed by a bullet. Although he was briefly deemed a quadriplegic, today he has limited use of his left arm and can't move the fingers on the left hand. But, that hasn't stopped him from being viewed as a go-to guy for high profile clients.

The meeting that Frongillo called for was set, and it was agreed they would meet at a neutral site. When Fresolo went with Kiley to the address they had been given, he didn't recognize the building. Kiley advised Fresolo that it was unusual for such a meeting to be set with the two clients being present. But he did not anticipate any difficulty.

Fresolo and Kiley drove over the Seaport Boulevard Bridge and found a parking spot near the new One Marina Park building. They proceeded to the 13th floor and found the meeting room. Attorney Frongillo and Walsh took one side of the table and Kiley, and Fresolo took the other. Walsh started immediately to speak.

"John, if I ever thought that I would find myself in this position as Chairman of this committee investigating a fellow colleague, a friend, I would never have taken the chairmanship. I know none of us wants to be here, but the Speaker has directed us to proceed, and counsel wants to go over the process we intend to follow. If there were any way of avoiding all of this, I would welcome it."

Kiley spoke up.

"It's apparent that the Representative feels the allegations have no basis in fact and if we have to wait to make our case in the closed hearing we are prepared to do that. We continue to maintain that the Representative has a right to privacy that he is not willing to waive."

Counsel for the Committee, Frongillo responded to Kiley.

"We want to make it clear that we are prepared to present substantial evidence against the Representative. Some of this evidence may be highly embarrassing to the Representative."

"Are we to be allowed to see the evidence before the hearing?"

"We have records and documents that we have compiled and are continuing to compile. We will send it over to you for you to review."

"What are your intentions for scheduling the hearing? Will we have the hearing in the State House?"

"Yes, it will be in the State House. At this time, it will be quite soon. Perhaps in a couple weeks."

"Will we see who is to testify and who has been subpoenaed?"

"Yes, we will provide that."

Fresolo was trying not to let his discomfort show on his face. He listened to Attorney Frongillo deliver what he felt was a strident diatribe about the seriousness of the allegations and the claimed abundant evidence against him. He listened to the shrillness in Frongillo's voice as he continued to hammer that the evidence was highly embarrassing. What's the point of stating that over and over? Fresolo felt that his attorney had made it clear they were prepared to attend and participate in the hearing. What else is there to discuss?

Frongillo spoke up, "You may want to consider resigning to avoid the embarrassment that this evidence will present."

Fresolo was stunned. Where was his fair chance to explain things and make things right? Resign?

Fresolo blurted out, "I'm not resigning."

"You may want to reconsider that once you see the evidence."

"I'm not resigning. I'm a choir boy compared to what goes on at the State House."

Fresolo turned his stare from Attorney Frongillo to Walsh. Walsh lowered his head, and it was apparent he would not speak up. Fresolo knew that Walsh was as savvy as anyone about the way Representatives operated at the State House. Nothing he was doing was *not* a common practice among his colleagues, including Walsh.

"This woman is trying to destroy me. She must be psychotic. There is no truth to the allegations," said John.

Kiley cut in and directed his eyes and his question toward Frongillo.

"When can we expect to see this so-called evidence that is highly embarrassing to the Representative?"

"We will provide it in due course. It's still being compiled in some instances."

Frongillo turned back to Fresolo.

"It would be a mistake for you to put yourself through the hearing and have this evidence become public. You would do yourself a favor by resigning."

"I'm not resigning," blurted Fresolo. "I'm not resigning."

Fresolo shifted in his chair to sit sideways and looked past everyone to glance out the broad window at the city below. It was inconceivable to him how these vague allegations have culminated at this moment where his longtime colleague, Walsh, has deferred the conduct of the meeting to this high-priced lawyer, who knows nothing about how the State House works.

Kiley spoke up again.

"It doesn't seem right for counsel to direct comments toward the Representative about evidence he hasn't seen and to expect him to resign with nothing more than a list of unverified allegations."

"I'm not resigning," Fresolo chimed in. "I can't believe this is happening."

Kiley tried to get clarification on when the hearing would be held when the evidence would be submitted to him and whether Fresolo or counsel would be able to cross-examine witnesses.

Frongillo spoke up to say that the process had already been described and they would not vary from that plan. The evidence would be forthcoming.

It was clear that they would not yield on their standard, written process which prohibited cross-examination and participation by the accused's attorney.

As Fresolo sat and listened, he felt light-headed and couldn't form any thoughts to express how unfair this all sounded. How can she make allegations that have no merit and now Counsel for the committee is pressuring him to resign based on evidence he hasn't seen? His own lawyer was focusing on procedures and not on stopping the madness.

Before he realized it, Fresolo was outside the building standing next to the car in the parking lot. He couldn't remember coming down the elevator; it was as if he was transported from that meeting room to the ground. It was hot outside, and he was sweating, something he couldn't control.

"Was this a choreographed act to get me riled up, to threaten me with releasing embarrassing stuff, to get me to resign?"

Kiley responded, "Well, John, this shows you who your friends are."

Fresolo thought to himself, Kiley is right. Walsh had sat there and never opened his mouth after Frongillo started barking at him. Had Frongillo deliberately tried to put the fear of God into him about how things would turn out if he went ahead and let the committee hold the hearings? He felt he had threatened him. That's it. He had threatened to embarrass him and make his life a living hell. What else was it? How could you interpret it any other way?

Kiley and Fresolo were still standing in the parking lot. Fresolo didn't know if he was sweating because it was an unusually warm spring day or that Frongillo had gotten to him?

Kiley asked, "John, what do you want to do?"

"I'm not resigning. How can I?"

"Alright then, let's go after the bastards."

Thursday, May 9, 2013

Kiley was frequently communicating with Frongillo on matters of evidence, subpoenas, scheduling, and other tactical issues associated with the upcoming hearing. In a series of emails, the two attorneys kept a dialogue going in final preparations for the start of the hearing. Subpoenas are an important part of fact-gathering as it allows both sides of the question to control time and place for witnesses and testimony. The State had agreed to issue a subpoena to Representative John Binienda as Kiley and Fresolo considered his testimony as crucial to their case.

Frongillo responded to Kiley's request, "if the purpose of the subpoena was to obtain the per diem records of

Representative Binienda, the House will obtain those documents and provide them to you."

Fresolo knew that he had to have access to the Binienda records so that a clear picture could be shown of how many per diem days were accounted for between them.

Kiley had become anxious about the timing of the subpoenas as it was almost a month since the House had authorized subpoenas to be sent. Frongillo finally sent an email that stated, "Chairman Walsh has signed most of the subpoenas that you requested on behalf of Representative Fresolo. They can be picked up tomorrow morning at Jim Kennedy's office (Office of Legal Counsel) after 9:00 AM."

The next notice was of great significance. It stated, "The Committee will serve the subpoena for Representative Binienda."

This was good news for Kiley and Fresolo. It was important to them that Binienda is compelled to appear at the hearing. His rate of filing for per diem reimbursement mostly paralleled Fresolo's and in recent years had exceeded the rate of claims made by Fresolo. Testimony and records demonstrating this would ensure that the committee members realized that these two colleagues were eager and frequent travelers to Boston throughout the year. Binienda was considered by most in the State House as the third most powerful member behind the Speaker and the Majority Leader. He chaired the influential Rules Committee and was not above using his position to muscle people on behalf of the Speaker and himself. His testimony would carry great weight for those conducting the hearing.

Subpoenas were prepared and sent to friendly witnesses that Fresolo requested to appear on his behalf at the hearing. The subpoena made it simple for everyone as the date, time, and place was controlled, allowing for a smooth process for those giving testimony and for the committee members.

According to final planning by the committee, the target date to start the next Executive Conference was on or about Tuesday, May 14 or Wednesday, May 15, 2013. Although the start of the hearing had been long anticipated, the actual notice to participants was now quite short. It was already May 10, and the hearing might start as soon as next Tuesday. This put a rush on everyone to get ready; committee members, the attorneys, and the witnesses for the State and for Fresolo.

Chapter Five

Witness for the State

Wednesday, May 15, 2013

Chairman Walsh looked around the room and surveyed that all the committee members were on hand, in their places, with name tags affixed to the broad dais that they would sit behind. Out front were two tables with microphones, one for John Fresolo and his Attorney, Thomas Kiley, and the other table for each witness that would come in to be sworn, and then answer questions from the committee.

In having not compromised with Fresolo's attorney on the question and cross-examination process, Walsh was now confident he could keep control of the hearing and move more quickly without any interference from counsel on process, procedures, and tactics. Walsh wanted to maintain control, and he had it now.

The 11 members of the committee all had copies of the letters, documents, and preliminary reports that had been prepared by the Office of Legal Counsel. They had received them at the first Executive Conference on April 9. At that brief meeting, they had informed Fresolo and his attorney how things would proceed.

It had been five months since Ryan had been married and went on her honeymoon and Fresolo had been re-elected, unopposed in his district, for the eighth consecutive term. It had been only 62 days since Ryan had finally shown Attorney Fleming of the Office of Legal Counsel the infamous photograph of Fresolo's penis. In the next very few days, Fresolo's biggest personal crisis would finally play out. No one knew what to expect.

Instead of continuing to nurture their political careers Ryan and Fresolo would meet face-to-face in an adversarial setting of a political kangaroo-court administered by a Chairman who had never been a chairman and had no legal background or training in ethics beyond the in-house coaching provided by the House Leadership office.

Two powerhouse attorneys were in the room as this was the battleground they commonly worked in. One was bearing down on behalf of the State with an eye toward establishing himself with his new law firm and more potential work from the State. The other was tethered to his chair, unable to use his skills as an examiner of witnesses, more immobilized than his partially paralyzed arm and fingers. Would this or could this be a fair fight for Fresolo?

Chairman Walsh spoke up.

"May I have everyone's attention, please? This session of the Executive Conference of the House Ethics Committee will come to order.

Walsh softly tapped the gavel to gain attention, which he got immediately.

"I want to thank all of the members of the committee for appearing this afternoon and if there is no objection we can get started. First, I would like our counsel, Mr. Frongillo, to please read the list of particulars that are contained in the report provided by the Office of Legal Counsel."

Attorney Frongillo was seated along with the committee at the bench overlooking the hearing room. He read from the binder that had been distributed to everyone in the room.

"In the matter of the charges that are before us concerning Representative John Fresolo, The Office of House Counsel has concluded that there is sufficient cause to warrant further investigation by the appropriate authority into the following 13 allegations:

1. Representative Fresolo used his House of Representatives email account to send or attempt to send nude photographs of his genitalia to a female who is not the complaining witness.

2. Representative Fresolo used his House of Representatives email account to log onto a Facebook page wherein he appears to have exchanged instant messages of an explicit sexual nature with other females who were not the complaining witness.

3. Representative Fresolo actively employs an administrative aide in his district who works fewer hours than what the aide is paid for, has no House of

Representatives email address, and whose pay stubs were often delivered to Representative Fresolo.

4. Representative Fresolo directed employees to perform campaign work during normal business hours.

5. Representative Fresolo used his official position and state resources to help his sister alter and postpone her jury duty services.

6. Representative Fresolo used his official position and state resources to assist his daughters in obtaining employment and college placement.

7. Representative Fresolo applied pressure in connection with certain recommendations for employment made by Representative Fresolo.

8. Representative Fresolo assisted his niece in obtaining a job at a state agency.

9. Representative Fresolo assisted his nephew in obtaining a job at a state agency.

10. Representative Fresolo assisted his uncle in obtaining a job at a private company.

11. Representative Fresolo assisted his brother in getting his brother's plumbing business on NSTAR's preferred vendor list.

12. Representative Fresolo filed inaccurate per diem reports, inflating the number of trips he made to the State House.

13. Representative Fresolo obtained concert tickets from TD Banknorth Garden."

Upon completing the reading of the allegations, Frongillo then described how the hearing would proceed. The State had a series of witnesses that would testify regarding specific allegations with which they had information, and the committee members would be able to ask questions. When the State had completed its presentations to the committee, Representative Fresolo would have the opportunity to present witnesses to provide testimony on any allegation with which they had information the committee could consider.

Chairman Walsh said, "Alright, thank you, Mr. Frongillo. Before we get to the first witness I want to ask you, John, would you like to make a statement to the committee?"

Fresolo was not ready for this.

No one had said he could make an opening statement. He hadn't thought to ask for that right, and now he was unprepared. He had no notes.

"Yes, Mr. Chairman. Thank you. First, I can't believe this is happening. These charges don't make any sense. I don't know why she's doing this to me. I've always been good to her. I've gone out of my way to let her have time off when she needed it. I don't understand why she's making these allegations."

Because Fresolo had not prepared any remarks for this occasion, already, he realized he was rambling and simply playing the role of the innocent victim of a bully. He sounded weak and not in command of the situation, which he was not.

Fresolo couldn't help himself, he continued, "This girl is a nightmare. I'm sorry for being emotional. I was good to her. You don't understand what it's like to drive up to my house and find the TV stations on my lawn. The press is running articles filled with lies and inaccuracies. My family has to see this stuff on TV."

Since the first TV reporting and newspaper headlines a month ago, the city had endured the Boston Marathon bombing and the subsequent continuous media coverage of its aftermath. Fresolo's family did not see anything on TV about his situation. It had drifted down to the back pages of some blogs and appeared almost nowhere else. The committee members could hear the anguish in his voice, but they hardly believed his family was suffering from overexposure on TV.

Fresolo was repeating the same weak comments he had made at the initial Executive Conference more than a month ago, which he and his attorney had jointly concluded had not gone well. Fresolo continued in the role of victim and did not take stock of the situation that presented itself for him to make an impression that he was a loyal colleague of everyone on the committee and that they should empathize with his situation. He was not connecting with anyone, and he knew it. He pivoted to his stump speech, which played so well in the District.

"I've always worked hard for my District. I've never done anything to hurt anybody, and for people now to think things because of these false allegations, well, it's just not right."

Chairman Walsh detected that Fresolo was finished. It seemed a bit brief to him, but he was prepared to move on.

"Mr. Frongillo, where shall we begin?"

"Mr. Chairman, with your permission, I would like to make a brief presentation that addresses the Allegation number 12 regarding inflated per diem requests. We have a few exhibits to present, and if we could have the lights dimmed, we can begin."

Frongillo and his legal team had spent the past month tabulating, analyzing, calculating, and plotting numbers gathered from cellphone records, transponder records, credit card records, email messages, State House access card records, EZ Pass records, and other similar sources including roll-call voting records to compile a profile of how many visits John Fresolo had made to Boston from his home in Worcester. The Microsoft PowerPoint slideshow that he had prepared was 46 pages of charts encased in a spiral-bound binder with a heavy mil clear plastic cover. A copy of the presentation was distributed to all committee members. It was labeled as Exhibit 15 for the Executive Conference on May 15, 2013.

The exhibit displayed 36 individual months between January 2010 and December 2012. The very first exhibit, for January 2010, was completely incomprehensible.

The legend at the side of the full-color chart indicated that there were 8 days they agreed he was in Boston and 11 days claimed that the State viewed as "unaccounted for." Yet, on five of those 11 days, it was clearly evident that he had passed through the Allston/Brighton Interchange on those dates. How do you pass through the Interchange and not be on the way to Boston?

Fresolo looked at the chart, and it occurred to him that the other unaccounted dates were days he was in Bineinda's car. Don't they understand that?

Fresolo called out, "Mr. Chairman, of course, this is unclear because you didn't have Binienda's trips for that month when I was in *his* car."

Chairman Walsh instructed Fresolo he was out of order and to let Counsel continue with its presentation.

Fresolo thought to himself, out of order? They've got crap information 10 feet high on the screen, and *I'm* out of order?

Another example of inconsistent data was May 2010, which had three dates where, due to phone data that appeared to originate in Worcester, the State said someone else must have been driving through the Allston/Brighton Interchange on those dates. Again, Fresolo is thinking to himself, who's driving in his car day after day into Boston, if it isn't him?

For January 2011, the State shows four dates claimed for per diem and the EZ Pass records show the car traveling to Boston. Yet, the State claims it has phone calls originating from Worcester on the same date. The data on the phone calls continues to be inconsistent and deemed unreliable.

Attorney Frongillo took the committee page by page through the report using the remote control to chart forward slide by slide. Many of the slides showed the same relative number of confirmed days and the same number of unaccounted for days by their reasoning. Frongillo lingered on some slides and went into detail and on others, he passed over quickly.

As John sat and listened to the presentation, he wondered why they hadn't included John Binienda's data in the charting? Without Binienda's data, it would not be possible to see the total number of days that Fresolo was in Boston – or for that matter – how many days Binienda was in Boston. No matter, Binienda should be able to clarify this when he testifies to the committee.

Frongillo continued with the presentation of slides. After reviewing a few more slides, Representative Jay Barrows (R-Mansfield) spoke up.

"Excuse me, Mr. Chairman. Counsel has just shown a calendar month with 15 days that the Rep's car was in Boston, but his phone was pinging in Worcester. He only has one phone, so it's reasonable that he's in Boston and the phone record makes no sense."

Frongillo stepped away from the screen and moved toward the dais to face Representative Barrows.

"I know, Representative, but it's something we can't account for."

"What do you mean you can't account for it?"

"We admit there are some inconsistencies in the tracking data. But, the only thing I can say, or that we have come up with is that Representative Fresolo let someone use his car and more than likely it's that he let someone use his car and park at the State House while he remained in Worcester."

Fresolo almost lost his mind when he heard that wild preposterous reply to a totally legitimate question raised by Barrows.

Fresolo blurted out, "Yeah, that's right, I let someone else take my car, drive to Boston 15 or 20 times? Come on, Mr. Chairman?"

Barrows spoke up, "Mr. Chairman, that explanation doesn't sound right, that's not too convincing. It's hard to believe he'd do that."

Frongillo continued, "we admit that it doesn't add up correctly, but overall, we see a pattern of claims that don't match the records of dates he was in Boston."

Suddenly, Rep. Matthew Beaton (R-Shrewsbury) spoke up.

"Yeah, that's not right," said Beaton.

Frongillo further acknowledged that despite these and other inconsistencies in the records, he believed that what he was presenting was factual.

Fresolo was taken up short by the sudden defense launched by two Republicans that were not really close colleagues of his. They had listened to the presentation and read the charts, and it was not convincing. Taken with the widely known co-riding habits of Binienda and Fresolo, similar to many other Legislators, it was easy to see why data records would not match actual dates that someone was in Boston. The evidence presented by Frongillo on behalf of the State was highly suspect in their minds.

Given that Frongillo and his team had committed many hours of work to prepare the report he plunged ahead and reviewed all three years of records and presented some summary slides that showed their estimate of alleged overreporting by Fresolo. A quick check of the math showed that even if you fully accepted the State's count for unaccounted days, the Representative overcharged by less than $15,000 for the three years.

Fresolo quipped to himself that the legal bill for this report was probably ten times that amount.

There were few follow-up questions after the comments made by Representative Barrows and Beaton. When Frongillo was finished showing the slides, Chairman Walsh polled the committee, and it was agreed they would adjourn for the day and reconvene the next morning.

Fresolo turned to Kiley and said he was surprised that the two Republicans had spoken up questioning the validity of the data. Kiley said that all of the Representatives should be concerned that sloppy forensic work such as was just displayed could put many or all of them in trouble at some point in the future. That could account for them challenging the presentation on its accuracy.

Thursday, May 16, 2013

Officially, today was the third day of the Executive Conference. It was the second day this week that the committee had convened and would continue taking testimony. Chairman Walsh called the session to order and turned to Attorney Frongillo to indicate who today's first witness was?

Frongillo said the first witness was Laura Richter, an aide in a nearby office to Representative Fresolo. He said that she was called in the matter of the allegation that Representative Fresolo had sent a nude photograph of himself to someone using the State House computer system.

The court officers assigned to assist with the Executive Conference today brought Laura Richter into the hearing room where she took a seat at the witness table.

Chairman Walsh addressed the witness.

"Ms. Richter, please give your full name and your position here in the State House."

"My name is Laura Richter, and I work as an aide in the State House."

Chairman Walsh then told Richter that he was going to administer the oath to her and that he and any of the committee members who chose to would ask her questions about the allegation in question.

When he had finished with administering the oath, Walsh said, "Ms. Richter, would you please tell us how it was that you came to see the photograph that Representative Fresolo had taken and was on the State House computer?"

"Yes, sir. I work in an area close to where Jamie Ryan works, and we have known each other for quite a while. On this day, Jamie came to me and asked me to accompany her back to her office area. She opened up the computer screen and showed me the message that contained the photograph."

"What did you do when you saw the photograph?"

"At first, I was surprised, not sure what I was looking at. Then when I realized what it was, I think I laughed. Maybe a stifled laugh."

"How did Jamie Ryan describe what this was and where it came from?"

"She actually didn't. It was clear that it was a text message from someone to someone else and because Jamie had access to the system, she could see it."

"What happened then?"

"Nothing. We viewed the photo and the message with some derisive amusement, and that was that. I went back to my office, back to work."

At this moment, Fresolo drew up his attention, which had been wandering all of last night and all morning since watching all of those slides yesterday. Now, he was listening to some young woman from the next office telling how the picture of his private parts had been shown around the office by Ryan to others; but that Ryan had never thought to help him out by showing him it was there and that something must be wrong for it to be there. She confided in others but not in him.

Fresolo turned to his attorney and whispered, "What did she say, derisive?"

"Derisive amusement."

"What the hell is that?"

"It means to be bemused, to laugh at something. They giggled when they saw the picture," said Kiley.

"They laughed? But, Jamie told House Counsel it made her vomit."

"John, there is what *actually* happened, and there is what she claimed happened."

Chairman Walsh asked a few questions to determine if Richter or Ryan had expressed concerns to each other about

Representative Fresolo's behavior toward either of them? Did she have any issues with the Representative or any of his behavior?

"No, I have no issues with him on that. I just saw what Jamie saw, and that was that."

Chairman Walsh asked if any other committee member had a question for Richter. Hearing none, he thanked the witness, and he addressed her with a comment.

"I would like to remind you that you should not discuss any of your testimony with any of the other witnesses. Thank you for coming today."

Richter rose from the table and was escorted out by the court officer.

Thursday, May 16, 2013

Chairman Walsh consulted his witness list and directed the court officer to bring in Annie Martin-McDonough, a former aide to Fresolo. She took a seat at the witness table, and Chairman Walsh administered the oath.

"Please state your name for the record."

"My name is Annie Martin-McDonough."

"Ms. Martin, I understand that you were an aide to Representative John Fresolo previously. Would you tell us when that was and how you came to work for him?"

"Yes, Mr. Chairman. I was working as an aide to a Representative who left office in early 2011, so I looked for another position and came to work for Representative Fresolo for two months in 2011."

Chairman Walsh caught everyone off guard with his first question.

"Did Representative Fresolo ever sexually harass you?"

Immediately, Martin said, "No, he never did anything like that."

"Did the Representative ever do or say anything that made you uncomfortable?"

"No, he did not."

"Alright, if you will please tell us about working with Representative Fresolo, what was it like?"

"Well, it was awkward for me as I quickly realized I didn't want to work for him."

"Why was that?"

"Well, it actually started in the interview for the job. He asked me if I would be okay working for him, given the things written about him if I went to Google. He asked did I plan to run against him. Things like that made it awkward."

"You took the job anyway?"

"Yes, but I was fortunate that I found out about another position and decided to leave and take the other job."

"What made you want to leave working for Representative Fresolo?"

"For example, he filed per diem claims when he hadn't come in on the days he claimed. He also wanted me to lie to a news reporter, Janet Wu, and I told him I wouldn't lie for him."

Fresolo turned to his attorney and whispered, "That's insane. During the six weeks, she was in my office, I filed no

197

per diem claims. None. She never filled out anything about per diems. She doesn't know what I submitted."

Kiley whispered back, "She's just going off things she read in the newspapers."

"That's not right. Can't we call her on that?"

"No, we just have to make our case later with other witnesses."

Chairman Walsh continued with the questioning.

"You said the Representative lied. What lie did he ask you to make?"

"He had an appointment to be interviewed on TV. He wanted me to tell Janet Wu that his daughter had been in an automobile accident and he couldn't do the scheduled interview that day. I told him I wouldn't lie for him."

Fresolo sat bolt upright in his seat and blurted out, "Mr. Chairman, that's just not true. I didn't ask her to lie about anything. I asked her to cancel the appointment for me, and she prompted me to know why I was doing that. Not that it was any of her business, but I told her my daughter had been in an accident and to tell Janet Wu that."

Fresolo was now on his feet and walking toward the dais. He had a stack of papers in his hand, which he started to pass out to the committee members.

"Mr. Chairman, this is a copy of the accident report that day. It became an insurance claim, and you can read the details. I did not ask the witness to lie about anything. But, she continues to make these statements."

Chairman Walsh and the other committee members reviewed the document, and Walsh turned to the witness.

"We can clearly see there was an accident. How are we to best understand your statement that the Representative asked you to lie?"

Martin-McDonough flustered for the moment did not respond. Taking a look at the piece of paper, she finally said, "Well, I thought that it was something he made up. I don't know."

"Alright, Ms. Martin, if there are no more questions from the committee, you are dismissed, but let me remind you not to discuss any of your testimony with the other witnesses."

Martin-McDonough got up, and the court officer escorted her out.

"Take that bitch," whispered Fresolo to Kiley.

Thursday, May 16, 2013

The next witness to be called by Chairman Walsh was Representative Jason Lewis, of Winchester, who was a Democrat representing the 31st Middlesex District. He was in his third term. His State House office space put him near Fresolo's office.

Earlier in the day, Lewis had been confronted by a news reporter seeking information about the on-going hearings. According to published reports, Lewis admitted he was testifying, but when the reporter sought more information, Lewis was hustled away by court officers, which reminded him he was not permitted to speak to the media without legal counsel present.

Chairman Walsh directed the court officers to bring the Representative to the hearing room. When he arrived, the Chairman administered the oath and directed some questions to him about Fresolo's attendance.

"Representative Lewis, I understand that you brought information to the Office of Legal Counsel regarding your knowledge of Representative Fresolo's attendance at the State House. Can you elaborate on that?"

"Yes, Mr. Chairman, I will do that. Along with others who heard about the questions that had been raised concerning possible inflated per diem requests, I found it curious that my personal observations contradicted the claims that Representative Fresolo made for travel days."

"Specifically, if you can, how do you know he inflated his claims?"

"It's based on my observations that compared with the number of days reported in the newspapers, it's my opinion that he was not in as often as he claimed. I am mostly here Tuesday through Thursday, and he's not here as much as I am."

Fresolo was listening to the testimony and wondering if Lewis is only in the office three days a week, how does he know what happens on Monday and Friday? It was as common for Fresolo to be in on those days of the week as any other. Lewis admits he wasn't there 40 percent of the time, so how can he count how many days anyone else is in? Fresolo could not contain himself.

"Mr. Chairman! This guy is *never* in the office! Why don't you check *his* per diem, shouted Fresolo; he's never in the office!"

Lewis responded, "Mr. Chairman, I don't take any per diem."

The comeback from Lewis caught Fresolo by surprise. He hadn't considered that not everyone takes per diem. In fact, the record shows that 25 percent of the Representatives take no per diem, generally because they live so close to the State House that it's an insignificant amount. Fresolo now realized that even though Lewis was not in very often by John's observation, because Lewis made no claim for per diem, it didn't matter.

Chairman Walsh turned his question to another topic with Lewis. He asked him about the photograph of Representative Fresolo.

"What do you know about the photo of Representative Fresolo?"

"I know that my aide had seen it and she told me about it."

"She told you about it?"

"Yes, she told me that Jamie Ryan had found it and she told me that she had seen it."

"Have you seen it?"

"No, I have not seen it."

"What did you do about it?"

"I didn't do anything. My aide told me about it and said that Jamie was trying to get a transfer out of that office, and she didn't want to cause anyone any trouble.'"

"Was it your intent that nothing should be done about this?"

"I wasn't sure what could be done as it was not my employee and I hadn't seen anything directly myself."

"I understand."

Chairman Walsh checked to see if any other committee members had further questions for Representative Lewis. Hearing none, he dismissed Lewis and reminded him that the committee's instructions were that witnesses not discuss testimony with anyone.

Lewis made a sarcastic smirk in the direction of Fresolo as he turned to leave the room.

Chairman Walsh called for a brief recess and gave a time for the committee to reconvene to hear more testimony. The next witness would be Ryan, the complainant that had launched the entire investigation and around whom many questions loomed as to why she was making these allegations at all.

Fresolo consulted with Kiley about how the first part of the day's hearing had gone. He felt that Lewis hurt the most with observations about attendance, but in reality, he had no evidence that would influence the committee other than opinion. As for the other witnesses, the one who accused Fresolo of wanting to tell a lie turned out to be the liar. The others had only confirmed that a photograph had shown up, but no one could say it was done deliberately to harass anyone. In fact, the witnesses stipulated that John had not sexually harassed them.

Thursday, May 16, 2013

When Ryan came into the room, she was accompanied by her Attorney, Joe Driscoll. No other witness had an attorney with them, and according to what the Office of

Legal Counsel had told her, she was entitled to have one, but it was not a requirement. As Jim Kennedy had told her during several of the interviews they had with her, as long as she was telling the truth, she had nothing to worry about.

Joe Driscoll was a former State Representative from Braintree representing the 5th Norfolk District for eight years. He last served as a Representative in 2011. He was in private law practice and was present today as Ryan's private counsel.

Chairman Walsh acknowledged Ryan and Driscoll and administered the oath to Ryan.

Walsh addressed Ryan and her Attorney.

"All of the committee members here today take the situation that has brought us here seriously. We understand that it was not easy to come forward and make these allegations, particularly because it involves your employer. We intend to have committee members ask questions, and then, in turn, will ask questions prepared by Representative Fresolo."

Fresolo listened as Walsh continued to lay down the ground rules for how the hearing would proceed, what the rules of questioning would be, and how he saw the afternoon proceeding. Immediately, Fresolo sensed that his inability to have his Attorney participate was going to handicap him in keeping control of the situation.

Chairman Walsh continued, "To begin with, and for the record, please give us your name and your position in the building."

"My name is Jamie Ryan, and I am an administrative aide for Representative Fresolo."

"How long have you worked for the Representative?"

"Two years."

"Ms. Ryan, has Representative Fresolo ever sexually harassed you?"

"Oh no, he's never done anything like that."

"He's not done anything that was in your mind inappropriate or of a harassing nature?"

"No, he's never done anything like that. He may call me 'hon' or something, but that's just annoying, not harassment."

Fresolo was startled by the questions Walsh was asking. He sensed that everyone else in the room was startled too. What was the basis for asking about sexual harassment? There was no allegation about that. Was he trying to pin lewd behavior on him? Or, was he trying to set straight that he had not done anything unacceptable as might have been bantered around in newspaper headlines and general State House gossip? Fresolo was not sure what to think.

"I understand. Can you otherwise describe what he's like to work for? What the work environment is like?"

"He sometimes asked me to do things that made me uncomfortable."

"Things like what?"

"He had me make phone calls to help his relatives get jobs."

"Did you feel like you were pressuring employers by making these phone calls?"

"It was the calling over and over again that made it feel like it was pressure."

"Did he ask you to call on behalf of people who were not his relatives too?"

"Yes, there were people who were not qualified, I thought, for the jobs that we were asking about."

"Ms. Ryan, you went to the Office of Legal Counsel to report that you had found a photograph, a nude photograph, on the Representative's computer. Can you tell us how this happened and why you reported it?"

"Last November, when I returned to work after my honeymoon, I had to follow-up on old emails that had gone unanswered since I left. When I checked the sent folder of an item, that the Representative wanted, I found the message with the photograph."

"Did this photograph appear to be sent to you by the Representative?"

"No, it was addressed to (Jane Doe)."

"What did you do about the photograph?"

"I didn't do anything."

"Didn't you show it to someone?"

"Yes, I showed it to a co-worker who sits near me."

"Why did you do that?"

"I didn't know what to do about it,"

"Did you think the Representative was doing something wrong?"

"Yes, he was using the state computer against the rules not to use it for anything that was not state business."

"Did you think the Representative wanted you to see it?"

"No, he didn't want me to see it."

"You've come to understand that he claims he didn't use the computer at the office, that the picture was sent late at night and from his cell phone?"

"Yes, I have heard that now."

"What else can you tell us?"

"He sent inappropriate messages."

"When you say inappropriate messages, were they inappropriate for the person to whom he sent them?"

"What do you mean?"

"If he sent them to you, and you didn't want to see them, that might be inappropriate, but if he sent it to someone who was responding the same way, would that be inappropriate?"

"I don't know."

"Okay, let's move on. Ms. Ryan, you reported that the Representative had a no-show employee. Why did you feel that way?"

"He said he was his aide in the district, but I never saw him, or only saw him once and never worked on anything with him."

"Did him not working with you make your job harder?"

"No, it's just that it didn't seem right that we didn't see him. He didn't have an email address."

"You didn't know that his district aide had worked for him over 10 years?"

"No, I did not."

"Let's turn to something else. You said you were uncomfortable about some things the Representative asked you to do, but how was he as a boss? Didn't he give you time off when you asked?"

"Yes, he was good on that. He gave me time off."

"Did he let you work from home when you asked?"

"Yes, he did."

"You reported that he left an angry message when you didn't call him back right away, was that something he did often, leave angry messages, get angry with you?"

"No, that was not how he acted. It was that time that he got angry."

"Alright, that's what I have, do any of the members of the committee have a question for Ms. Ryan?"

Representative Peter Kocot (D-Northampton, 1st Hampshire District) spoke up.

"Mr. Chairman, I have a question. Jamie, now please don't take this the wrong way. I know you have been through a lot. But, I need to ask you a question that's bothering me. You said John was a good guy to work for. He let you go and come as you wanted up until these last couple weeks where he had issues with you not returning calls. But, as far as the picture goes, you saw it five months ago. You said you saw it in November, and you didn't bring it to the House Counsel's attention until March, is that right?"

"Yes, that's right."

"Can you just answer me why wouldn't you just go to him and say, 'Hey Rep, you may want to look at this and do something about it,' because you said he was a good guy to work for, wouldn't you?"

The fidgeting in the room that accompanied a lot of the back and forth during testimony had stopped. The small clusters of members leaning side to side to make remarks to each other and whispering while questions were asked and answered all stopped. Everyone was poised for the answer to the question everyone in the room had on their minds.

At that precise moment, Ryan burst into tears at the witness table, dropped her head down into her hands, and began weeping openly. The tension in the room swelled.

This breakdown was unexpected, but maybe it shouldn't have been. Despite her occasional denials, she was well-known to weep or get misty at the smallest provocation, and this was no small provocation. She was accusing her employer of the past two years of 13 examples of unethical behavior that could earn him a censure, punishment, and banishment from the 15 years he had devoted to his elective office.

Now, under questioning, Ryan, could not hold in her emotions.

Her Attorney spoke up.

"Mr. Chairman, may we ask for a brief recess for my client to compose herself?"

"Yes, surely, of course, let's take a 10-minute break and then we will reconvene."

Chairman Walsh tapped the gavel, and everyone rose to move toward the exits. Ryan and her Attorney continued to sit at the table while he tried to comfort her and help her recover. They then both rose and left the room.

Fresolo had seen this act before. Ryan was inclined to get misty eyes and weep openly when things got difficult for her. She was sensitive and unsure of herself in many ways. This was in contrast to her tendency to step up and take control of things by plunging into a task and asking permission for it after it was done. This is how many of the things that put Fresolo in jeopardy had started. She would be bold on the one hand and then melt away when challenged. It was a mercurial pattern that Fresolo never totally unraveled. He had not learned how to manage her so that she could be effective for him and for herself.

The recess lasted about an hour. The committee members had resumed their seats and the witness, her Attorney, and Fresolo and his Attorney took their seats.

Chairman Walsh reconvened the Executive Conference now that Ryan had composed herself and indicated she was ready to continue with her testimony. Her Attorney thanked the committee for its indulgence, and Chairman Walsh addressed Ryan.

"We will continue with the portion of the questioning using questions prepared by Representative Fresolo and submitted in writing. I will read the question and ask that you please respond to each question as fully as you can. Do you understand?"

"Yes, sir, I do."

"Okay, I will start with the first question."

"Did Representative Fresolo ask to talk to you about three or four different people who talked to the Representative about calling the office two or three times, left messages over a couple of days and never received a call back?"

"Yes, he spoke to me."

"Did the Representative tell you he didn't believe your answer, which was – it's just not true, it's just not true?"

"But it wasn't true."

"The three or four people did not know each other, and they said the same complaint, and Representative Fresolo told you they don't know each other, and they are saying the same thing. Is that true?"

"I don't remember."

"Did Representative Fresolo tell you that you are taking five or six cigarette breaks a day besides your lunch hour and very frequent breaks to get something to eat, and you need to be at your desk more than you are?"

"I'm at my desk and only take a few breaks."

"Did the Representative say to you – 10 minutes down, 10 minutes for the cigarette, 10 minutes to walk back, that's 20-30 minutes minimum. If I give you the benefit of the doubt, four breaks a day, that's two hours you're not at your desk - Is that true?"

"I don't take that many breaks."

"Did Representative Fresolo call you and you were outside the building somewhere, and he asked where you were? Did you say – In the building – and did the Representative say – you are not in the building, you are outside?"

"I was not outside."

"Did the Representative ask you if you transferred your phone to get calls from the desk phone?"

"Yes, he asked me that."

As Fresolo sat and listened to the exchange between Walsh and Ryan, it sounded completely different than what had happened during the earlier questioning period with Ryan. Her demeanor previously had been more expansive, if not helpful in answering the questions. But now, she was like a robot. She gave simple, clipped answers, sometimes just a word or two. And, now that Walsh was reading the questions, which he had not previously seen, his delivery was stilted and monotonous, making it sometimes hard for Fresolo to recognize his own questions. What had happened?

Speculating on the change, was it possible that her Attorney had told her that she needed to answer the questions simply and without elaboration? It was clear that no follow-ups were coming from committee members, and Fresolo and his Attorney, Kiley, were not permitted to make follow-up questions. If he told her to just give the shortest, simplest answer possible, the questions would dry up, and it would be over.

Walsh continued reading the questions.

"Did the Representative leave the building and call you on the phone at the desk and not get you after trying four times unsuccessfully, and is that the occasion that you described to House Counsel as – I was away from my desk for 17 minutes and he left an angry message?"

"I don't know."

Walsh turned to another series of questions.

"Jamie, you said you were unhappy and wanted to transfer. Why didn't you ever talk to Representative Fresolo about how you felt?"

"I didn't know how he would take it."

"Did you feel that Representative Fresolo was hard to work for?"

"I was concerned about some things he asked me to do."

Fresolo's mind was racing again. This testimony sounded like it was coming from a completely different person.

Fresolo speculated that Joe Driscoll, Ryan's attorney, in trying to calm her down and help her regain her composure, had pointed out that she was not the person on trial here. No one was going to make allegations against her for the way she behaved. All she had to do was answer any questions as honestly as she could.

He probably reminded her that she already had a new job at the State House and that she was secure for the future, with her plans with her husband to buy a house and raise a family. All she needed to do was answer a few more questions, and the matter would be closed for her.

He might even have pointed out that after she answered any question, no one was following up with a second question. Each answer was taken as she gave it. No cross-examination was coming from the committee, and none could come from Fresolo or his Attorney. If the Chairman doesn't recognize Fresolo, he can't speak.

"When Representative Fresolo ever had people in his office, would you come in and sit and participate in the casual conversations with the visitors?"

"I did talk with visitors."

"How did Representative Fresolo dress when he came into the office? Did he wear a suit all the time? Did he ever wear street clothes in the office? Would he wear street clothes more often than a suit?"

"I'm not sure what you are asking," said Jamie.

Fresolo interjected, "Mr. Chairman, that's not the question, you have read it wrong."

"I've read it right, said Walsh. Did he wear street clothes?"

"He wore suits and street clothes."

Fresolo was getting frustrated. Walsh was clumsy in how he asked the questions. The point of this one was anyone who saw Fresolo saw him in casual clothes more often than a suit as he was there on many non-formal session days.

Walsh continued with the questions.

"Did you ever have lunch in Worcester at the Parkway Diner when you first started to work for Representative Fresolo with his many community activists and his eyes and ear in his district?"

"Yes, I went once to the Diner in Worcester when I first started."

"After that were you ever asked to come to Worcester for any work-related duties, if so, what, and if not, which is the case he handled all the district work, and you had no involvement, isn't that right?"

"Yes, that's right."

"Jamie, you said in your testimony to the House Counsel that Representative Fresolo's two daughters don't like him. Would you please explain why you feel that or would say that when you only have met them two or three times at functions?"

"I could tell by the way they spoke; they did not like him."

"If they were asked by someone if they told you that, would they say yes?"

"I don't know what they would say."

"In your testimony to the House Counsel, you stated that you told Paul Iannuccillo about the picture, but Iannuccillo does not state that in his remarks to the House Counsel. Did you or did you not tell him?"

"I don't remember."

"Jamie, you went to the House Counsel originally for fear of ethics violations that Representative Fresolo might ask you to perform. Why didn't you talk to Representative Fresolo about the new ethics reform before going down to House Counsel?"

"I didn't know how he would react."

"You also brought up the picture. The two items you brought to House Counsel turned into 14 items. Did House Counsel ask you to go back and think of anything else you can think of and come back, or did you do it on your own?

"I brought things on my own."

"The allegations you brought to House Counsel were two items. Then, the items went to seven at your second meeting, and by the third meeting, seven grew to 14 items. What was the reason for not bringing them to their attention the first meeting?"

"I didn't think of them at first."

"Jamie, you said today you were unhappy for a while, why wouldn't you have ever spoken to Representative Fresolo about it?"

"I wasn't sure how he would react."

Walsh turned to another series of questions relating to her wedding and other issues.

"Jamie, did Representative Fresolo ask you if you would mind if he didn't attend your wedding because he had a fundraiser scheduled for the next morning at 8 AM?"

"Yes, he mentioned the breakfast."

"Did you break into tears and say – Can't you come for just an hour?"

"I didn't break into tears."

"You didn't break into tears?"

"No."

"Did the Representative come to your wedding?"

"Yes."

"Did he sit with friends that you told him were employed with or supported Congressman Steve Lynch?"

"Yes."

"Did you ask Representative Fresolo who he was supporting in the US Senate primary and when he said – Steve Lynch – you said – Yes! – in excitement, because your friends at the wedding were obviously going to be supporting him?"

"He said he was supporting Steve Lynch."

Walsh turned the questioning to work schedule and other issues.

"Jamie, how many days a month would you ask to work from home. Was it one, two, five?"

"It wasn't that many."

"Did the Representative ever refuse you from working from home when you asked to do so?"

"No."

"The Representative heard you say you thought you were working – 24/7. Did he ever call you after 5:00 PM, or on weekends?"

"He sometimes called me."

"Representative Fresolo does not ever recall calling you after 5:00 PM or on weekends unless it was an emergency. In the two years you worked for him he can only account for one or possibly two times maximum. Is he right? If not, please explain when you would be called and how frequently?"

"I don't recall."

"Jamie, how many times are you late and are not here at 9:00 AM? Would you say Representative Fresolo was right if he said four out of five days?"

"I'm not late that often."

"Did it not become so consistent a problem that Representative Fresolo said or asked you to call him or text him if you were going to be late?"

"The only time I am late is if traffic is a problem."

"How many times did Representative Fresolo tell you if your work was done and all calls returned you could go home early, once or twice a week?"

"He let me go home early on occasion."

"Jamie, on Wednesday, March 6, did you ask Representative Fresolo to talk about a job opening in the Labor Workforce committee and did you say to him you wanted to apply and ask him – would you be pissed? Is that true?"

"I told him I wanted to apply."

"Did you say to the Representative – I can't believe you aren't pissed that I want to leave? Did he say no, he wasn't, and he understood you wanted to improve and have a job that could accrue time for maternity leave?"

"I didn't say I thought he would be pissed."

"Did you ask him to put in a – good word – for you with Chairman Conroy?"

"I asked him to."

"After his meeting with Chairman Conroy did you ask him if he put in a good word for you, and when he said he didn't have time, it didn't come up, what was your reaction."

"I went back to my desk."

"Two days later, on March 8, you went down to House Counsel with more allegations. Did the Representative failing to speak to Chairman Conroy spur you to go to the House Counsel?"

"No."

Chairman Walsh asked the few remaining questions, all of which received short, clipped non-answer answers and neither he nor any of the committee members added a follow-up question.

Walsh asked if there were any final questions or comments, and then he thanked Ryan and her Attorney and dismissed them.

Walsh closed the hearing for the day.

Friday, May 17, 2013

Today was the fourth day of the Executive Conference and the third day of testimony before the committee. Chairman Walsh indicated to the committee and Fresolo and Kiley that he appreciated everyone's patience and attendance and that the next witness would be the concluding witness for the State. When it was completed, Representative Fresolo would be asked to present his witnesses.

Chairman Walsh directed the court officers to bring in Keith Johnson of the Human Services department.

"Mr. Johnson, now that we have administered the oath I will tell you that you are here regarding an allegation made against Representative Fresolo about his District Aide, Ken

Simoncini. For the record, Mr. Simoncini was released from employment by the State two months ago on March 20th."

"I understand."

"Keith, can you tell what the procedure is for a legislative aide and a district aide, and what is different about each one regarding timesheets?"

"Yes, Mr. Chairman. An administrative aide is generally a full-time employee and is on assignment to a particular Representative working at the State House. A district aide can be a full or part-time employee on assignment to a Representative to work in the home district on behalf of the Representative."

"Can you describe the purpose of the timesheet that a district aide fills out each week?"

"Yes. The timesheet allows payroll to properly record the hours worked and to have a record of earned vacation time, holidays, and things like that."

"If Mr. Simoncini had fallen behind or stopped submitting timesheets, how is it that he continued to be paid for his basic part-time hours?"

"To accommodate the payroll process and to not delay checks, the office processes weekly pay in anticipation that it will get the paperwork submitted at a later time."

"Does that seem appropriate to issue pay without a signed timesheet?"

"It hasn't up to this time been a problem."

"In your interview with the Office of Legal Counsel, it was indicated that you were going to check to see if other district aides had not been filling out forms. Have you done that?"

"Well, Mr. Chairman, as I explained to Counsel at the time that would be a very manual process and quite time-consuming. It has not been done yet."

"Can you tell us at this time if anyone else has not been filling out timesheets on time?"

"Right now, I don't have that information in front of me."

"How do employees know about the requirement for signing a timesheet?"

"When a new employee is hired, we instruct them on the requirement to fill out the timesheet."

"Was Ken Simoncini told to fill out a timesheet?"

"Yes, he was."

"Why do you suppose he didn't?"

"It's been our experience that when someone has been a legislative aide for a while and then switches to be a district aide, they don't realize the requirement is different. The district aide must fill out a form. Sometimes they have to be prompted by our office or by the Representative."

"When did Mr. Simoncini start work as an aide?"

"My records, which I have here, indicated he started in 2006."

"Would he have been told at that time?"

"Yes, Mr. Chairman."

Fresolo could contain himself no longer.

He blurted out, "That's ridiculous. No one told Ken or me to fill out forms. No district aide that I had before Ken filled them out either."

"You're out of order, John," said Chairman Walsh.

"He's got his records there, ask him when he called me. He didn't."

"That's all, John. That's enough."

Johnson responded, "Mr. Chairman, we would have told them when they were first hired or by a telephone call."

Fresolo sat there not believing anything he heard. It was widely known and accepted that the payroll was flushed through and timesheets were an afterthought by some employees and mostly ignored by the others. The state didn't care how a Representative used an aide. They were given tasks and worked to meet the needs of the Representative, and as long as they were satisfied, no one cared.

Fresolo could hear a muffled sound in the background. It was Walsh asking Johnson questions and Johnson making up something on the spot. If an employee doesn't fill out a form – and no one asks him about it for years – is that the employee's issue – or the management's issue? Fresolo's inner voice was drowning out the questioning going on in the hearing room.

Hadn't Jim Kennedy ordered Johnson to bring back a month's worth of records? Has anyone seen them? Of course not, they don't exist. Fresolo forced himself to pay attention.

Chairman Walsh continued with more questions. It was clear that Johnson had nothing to contribute further about the payroll process, and no other committee members had further questions.

"Okay, Keith, thank you for coming in. Please remember that your testimony is not to be discussed with other anyone including other witnesses."

"Yes, Mr. Chairman. Thank you."

Johnson got up and left the room.

Chairman Walsh said, "We will begin with rebuttal testimony from Representative Fresolo next, but let's first take a recess."

Fresolo and Kiley conferred over Johnson's testimony. He hadn't made a case that convinced any committee member that lack of a timesheet meant anything special. And in point of fact, Simoncini had been gone now for two months. It seems if anyone was unhappy with how he was supervised by Fresolo or whether he did a good job, he was gone now, and the issue of a possible no-show job was moot.

Kiley pointed out that if firing him was not enough of a punishment as viewed by the committee, it might rise to another level if the allegations went further on to the state ethics commission. They might seek further retribution. As long as an agreement was reached between the committee and Fresolo, that likelihood was diminished.

Richard F. Wright

Chapter Six

Witness for the Defense

Friday, May 17, 2013

Fresolo had spent the past few weeks preparing for an opportunity to rebut the allegations that Ryan had raised to the Office of Legal Counsel and which had prompted the Speaker to call for the House Committee on Ethics to conduct this secret investigation. Still bewildered about why she had made the allegations, and not sure whether he was going to be treated fairly, Fresolo had made dozens of phone calls to help recruit and coordinate witnesses to come and testify about what they knew concerning various allegations.

His family members were all willing to help, and a few of his ardent supporters in the district were willing, but some of the Representatives and others were unwilling to become witnesses on his behalf. They had their own fish to fry, and they didn't want to be in the skillet for Fresolo against House Leadership.

His brother and his brother's son, his sister, his campaign manager, his neighborhood buddies, his activist colleagues, two court officers, and former aides were among those willing to help. They all planned to come to Boston and to wait patiently for their turn to take the oath and give testimony that disputed the false allegations made by his current aide. Fresolo had only formerly asked for one witness to be subpoenaed; Representative John Binienda. The state had agreed to issue a subpoena to Binienda.

All of the witnesses for Fresolo had been gathering into the waiting room next to the hearing room. All had been asked to arrive for a 9:00 AM start. For the next three hours, his witnesses sat at the tables in the room and chatted with each other. Suddenly, someone came into the room around noontime and told them the committee had recessed and that they could take some time to get lunch. There were no facilities in the building, so everyone went out to Bowdoin Street to the various restaurants to get something to eat. During the time they had waited, there was no food or water available for anyone; they were all very hungry and thirsty.

After the lunch break, everyone was readmitted to the waiting room, and for another hour or more, they continued to wait. Former Representative Rucho, who was in his 90s, spoke to some of the other witnesses to let them know he wanted to go first if it was possible; the waiting was becoming a strain for him. Sheila Trapasso approached one of the court officers to find out how soon they would be called in, but he had no information to share with her.

Eventually, a court officer entered the waiting room and asked all of the witnesses to follow him out to the corridor.

Once in the corridor, he positioned the entire group along the corridor behind some stanchions with ropes to create a holding area. This barrier prevented the witnesses from straying or for outsiders to approach them.

After another hour of standing in the corridor, Sheila approached one of the court officers and asked if a chair could be brought out to the corridor to accommodate the elderly Rucho who was experiencing some difficulty with the long wait. Reluctantly the court officer retrieved one chair, and Rucho got a chance to sit down. The others remained standing.

The allegation had been made that Representative Fresolo applied for more per diem than authorized by his attendance at the State House. Fresolo believed the presentation made by Counsel for the Committee had inaccuracies on dates and frequency of contradictions that he and his Attorney felt could be adequately explained.

One way was by enlisting the testimony of colleagues he traveled with; with State House employees who witnessed his presence, and by coincidence the frequent presence of retired State Representative John Rucho who enjoyed the glamour of traveling to Boston each day to mingle and commiserate with former colleagues. It was his practice, as he testified, to ride with Fresolo and Binienda up to three days a week or more, therefore, confirming their attendance.

Witness: John Rucho, former Representative

Fresolo was always impressed with Representative John Rucho's dedication to public service which included three terms as a Representative for the Main South section of Worcester and his impressive background as a combat Navy veteran of World War II where he participated in amphibious assault action at Iwo Jima, Okinawa, and the Marshall Islands. At the time of his testimony on behalf of John Fresolo, Representative Rucho was 91.

It was now mid-afternoon on Friday, May 17, 2013, and the committee had listened to two days of testimony from its witnesses. Now, Chairman Walsh began the portion of the hearing where Representative Fresolo was permitted to introduce witnesses who could address the allegations that had been made against him.

Fresolo went out to the holding area and took Rucho by the arm to lead him into the hearing room. He turned to face the group of witnesses that were patiently standing there.

"The committee is now ready for you each to answer questions about the topic you are familiar with. Each of you will go one at a time, and I will let you know when it's your turn. I appreciate your patience, I know it's been a long day for everyone, but we are going to move quickly starting now."

Fresolo turned to Billy Breault.

"When Representative Rucho is done, I will have you come in next, Billy."

Rucho took a seat at the witness table and was sworn in by Chairman Walsh.

Walsh spoke up, "Hello Representative Rucho, thank you for coming in today. We will try to keep our discussion brief and to the point."

Rucho replied, "I just want to be helpful, Mr. Chairman."

"I'm sure you will," said Walsh.

Walsh continued," Representative Rucho, it has been alleged that Representative Fresolo applied for more per diem reimbursement than his attendance warranted. What can you tell us about his frequency of travel to Boston?"

"I can tell you that the trip to Boson each morning was important to me. Representative Binienda and Fresolo were always willing to have me come along so that I could visit with my colleagues here. I would mostly stay in his office."

"How often did you travel with them?"

"Everyday."

"Well, specifically, did you travel on days of formal sessions or on days when there were no formal sessions?"

"I traveled with them every day. Two or three days a week, at least. Sometimes I had appointments when I couldn't go with them, but I mostly went every day."

"Did they pick you up?"

"Yes, we had places where they would meet me and take me along."

"Did you see Representative Fresolo's aide in the office?"

"Sure, but I never heard her complain about anything."

"Did you travel in the winter and well as the summer?"

"I went as often as I could. I'm not taking vacations or traveling much anymore, so the trip to Boston was good for me."

"Do any committee members have more questions?"

Hearing no questions, Walsh addressed Representative Rucho.

"Representative, we thank you for coming in today, and as a reminder, please don't share your testimony with the other witnesses. Thank you."

"You're welcome."

Representative Rucho returned to the witness waiting area.

Witness: William 'Billy' Breault

Fresolo addressed the Chairman.

"Mr. Chairman, my next witness is Mr. Billy Breault, who serves as the Chairman of the Worcester Main South Alliance for Public Safety. He is here to offer testimony regarding my District Aide and how they work together."

Fresolo walked to the hearing room door and stepped into the corridor. Fresolo motioned to one of the witnesses to come forward. It was Billy Breault, a longtime friend who resides in Worcester and is a well-known community activist associated with the Main South Alliance for Public Safety and the Main South Community Development Corporation.

Fresolo escorted Breault inside the hearing room and indicated for him to take a seat at the small table centered in the room. Fresolo assumed his seat alongside his attorney at a table off to the right side of the room facing the seated committee members.

Chairman Walsh addressed the witness.

"To get started, please give us your name and place of residence."

"My name is William Breault, and I live in Worcester."

"That's fine. If you would raise your right hand, I will administer the oath."

Chairman Walsh administered the oath and asked Breault to be seated.

"Mr. Breault, the allegation has been made to the committee that Representative Fresolo has an aide on the payroll who does not work. Can you elaborate on that for us?"

"Yes, I can. First, I'm not sure why anyone would say something like that about Ken. He's someone that I work with continuously. I speak to him as often as I speak to John, that is the Rep, and that's more often than I like to think about."

"In what way do you work with Mr. Simoncini, that is, what do you call him about?"

"I spend a lot of my time trying to get assistance for our neighborhood from the city and the state, and to make our case to the state, it's important to contact everyone involved. If I need to hold a meeting, I can ask Ken to set a place and time and then make calls to get folks to attend that we need. This can be calling the Rep, or the Mayor, or a Councilor that we want to discuss something with. It can be the police chief or others that may have an interest."

"Specifically, what does Mr. Simoncini do?"

"He's the person I call to ask John to contact someone at the State level. If I can't get John on the phone, I call for Ken. Ken will get the message to John, and then Ken will call me back to follow-up."

"How long have you known Mr. Simoncini?"

"He's been John's aide off and on over many years. I would guess several years. When he was not the district aide,

I would call whoever John had at the time. I've known John for over 15 years."

"Do you also call on the Representative's other aide, in Boston?"

"No, I don't. She's his administrative aide to handle typing and legislative items at the State House. I speak to Ken for community issues such as meetings, setting up interviews with local officials, holding community office hours. We used to hold them more regularly in the past, at places like the neighborhood centers, but it has been less often lately."

"How frequently do you talk with Mr. Simoncini?"

"I would say every week at a minimum. If something is about to happen or needs to be coordinated, we talk daily."

"Okay, I think that's all we have. Does anyone else have a question?"

Hearing none, the Chairman dismissed Breault with the admonition that he does not share or discuss his testimony with any of the other witnesses.

Breault left the hearing room and returned to stand and wait in the corridor with the other witnesses.

Witness: Ray McGrath

Fresolo addressed the Chairman.

"Mr. Chairman, the next witness is Mr. Ray McGrath, who is associated with NAGE. He is here to offer testimony on the help he provides to candidates in the form of printing invitations and brochures."

Ray McGrath was a legislative lobbyist on behalf of NAGE (National Association of Government Employees) and was a friend of Fresolo. McGrath was well known to everyone who sat on the ethics committee because it was his job to be in contact with legislators on behalf of a wide range of legislative issues before the House members that concern government employees including police, firefighters, correctional officers, and health care workers.

McGrath was admitted to the hearing room and sworn in. Chairman Walsh addressed the witness.

"Welcome, Ray, please tell us what you know about this matter."

"Thank you, Mr. Chairman. Over the years, it has been our practice to assist candidates for office that share our concern for the safety and health of our membership. One of the things we do to support candidates is to facilitate the printing of letters and invitations because we are fortunate to have a fine printshop at our headquarters in Quincy."

"Do you do this for free?"

"Yes, we provide the printing of candidate profile and invitation items at no charge to candidates who make the request. And as you know yourself, Mr. Chairman, each candidate is provided with an in-kind donation slip for proper reporting on their campaign finance reports."

"How do you get the material you need from the candidate, and how do you distribute the printed material?"

"It's generally easy for me to drop off printed items or to have them shipped to the candidate from Quincy. I'm frequently at the State House."

"Did Representative Fresolo's aide come to NAGE and drop off material and pick up printed items?"

"No, that wouldn't happen. It's too easy for me to pick up and drop off as I'm in contact with John and others frequently. His aide did not have to come to our office. John only had one or two events in a year."

McGrath added, "Also, I might add that as committee members are aware, this is all perfectly legal for us to do so."

None of the members of the committee offered further questions. Chairman Walsh thanked McGrath and dismissed him.

Fresolo tried to stifle the bemused smile on his face. How ridiculous to have to ask Ray McGrath to come in and explain to the committee something he did for virtually all of them as well? If they worked closely with NAGE in its mission, they got free printing too.

The reason Ray would go out of his way to "drop off" and "pick up" is because he wanted to put his hand on your shoulder and give you updates on NAGE and its needs. He certainly didn't want somebody's aide depriving him of that face-to-face with the Representative.

Ray returned to the corridor and then left the building.

Witness: Representative Brian Ashe

For all the years he served as a State Representative, Fresolo had shared his daily ride to Boston with his fellow colleague from Worcester, John Binienda. Binienda had shared rides with Bill Glodis in the years past and with others as a way to save money. In the early years, the pay was not great, and this was a simple way to make a little more money.

Over the years, the reimbursement had moved up from $18 a day to the current $36 a day. But, that was in recognition of the increasing cost of transportation, including vehicle depreciation, fuel, insurance, and maintenance. The per diem also covered those nights spent in hotels near the State House when sessions ran late into the night.

When Fresolo had a falling-out with Binienda over who to support for Speaker and how Binienda abandoned his early support for him to run for Senate, the ridesharing ended. But, Fresolo sought co-pilots whenever and wherever he could. Lately, he had been riding with Representative Brian Ashe (D-Longmeadow) when they knew meetings would run late.

Fresolo felt Ashe's testimony would reinforce that it was a strong habit to ride with others, and that would help show why there were gaps in electronic tracking of his vehicle. Ashe agreed to testify.

Fresolo addressed the committee.

"Mr. Chairman, my next witness is Representative Ashe who can testify on the matter of per diems."

Chairman Walsh welcomed Representative Ashe and administered the oath.

Walsh addressed Ashe.

"Are we to understand that you and Representative Fresolo share rides into Boston?"

"Mr. Chairman, yes, that's correct. Representative Fresolo suggested that as we both travel down the Turnpike that we can share a ride on occasions."

"How frequent was this?"

"In the past year, I picked up Representative Fresolo about 15 to 20 times."

"Do you share rides with anyone else?"

"Actually, no, it's just that we both go down the Turnpike and it's convenient."

"Okay, Representative, thank you. Is there anything else, Brian?"

"No, Mr. Chairman."

Walsh said, "Alright, I don't think there are any more questions."

Then another person spoke up.

"Ah, Mr. Chairman, I have another question."

Walsh's eyes darted over to Representative Paul Donato (D-Medford), who was breaking the unwritten rule not to put a colleague on the spot with a question.

Donato plunged ahead.

"Representative Ashe, you said you picked up John 15 to 20 times this year?"

Ashe responded, "Yes, that's right."

"Can you tell me what exit you picked him up at?"

"Yeah, I think it was 10A."

Turning his head toward where Fresolo was sitting, Ashe asked, "That's right isn't it John, 10A?"

Fresolo responded, "That's right. 10A."

Donato said, "Alright, Mr. Chairman, that's all I have."

Fresolo's mind raced, what was the point of asking that question? To try to show that Ashe was possibly making up a story about sharing rides with Fresolo by catching him not knowing the exit off the Turnpike? Fresolo was incredulous.

Chairman Walsh didn't ask if anyone else had a question and thanked Representative Ashe for coming in. He skipped the customary admonition to not share testimony with others.

Witness: Rocco Fresolo Jr. and Rocco Fresolo Sr.

Fresolo introduced his nephew (Rocky Jr.) to the committee to respond to the allegation that he had helped his brother (Rocky Sr.) get preferred status with NSTAR.

Rocco Fresolo Jr. was escorted into the hearing room and took his seat. Chairman Walsh administered the oath.

"I understand you have a prepared statement?"

"Yes, sir, I do. First, I am here today to discuss the situation that led to my appearance before this committee. A few months back, I was on a couple of service calls to repair heating system installations that were installed recently by others. After repairing the issues, I asked the customer who they had to install their new systems? They told me they were referred to the contractors through the Vendor List and told me I should get on it because I am more than qualified.

"They even went back into their records and found the list that they had received because I had no idea what they were even talking about. After looking through the paperwork I received, I called a couple of the numbers that were on the paperwork and asked how to be listed and what were the requirements? NSTAR told me all about it and said that we would be put on a waiting list. I discussed with my father the possibility that my Uncle John (Representative

Fresolo) might know anyone that could assist in placing me on this list. Also, my father discussed this list with other personal contacts that could assist as well.

"I would like to inform you of what this list represents. As stated by NSTAR paperwork given to prospective conversion customers, it states - These contractors are independent and not employees of NSTAR. NSTAR is not a party to any contract you sign with them and does not guarantee any work performed by them. You are under no obligation to use these contractors for your gas conversion.

"It also states - You should use a contractor of your choice and receive multiple estimates. When searching for an installer, you could also look in the Yellow Pages, ask neighbors and friends, focus on local companies, look for licenses and insured installers and inquire with the Better Business Bureau.

"These statements are taken directly from NSTAR paperwork that I have before me today. In conclusion, I would just like to state that this Vendor List is comprised of 13 other contractors. These are only potential sales leads, with the possibility if called to provide estimates on possible conversion from oil to gas. As of this date, we have provided estimates to potential conversion customers but have signed no contracts or performed any work for these private individuals. I am the general manager of our company and have taken over the day-to-day operations of this family-owned business. My father, Rocco Sr., although being aware of my desire to have our company placed on this list had no direct involvement with any phone calls or emails with this situation. Thank you."

"Okay, thank you for that statement. Does anyone have any further questions? Hearing none, then, I want to remind the witness that we ask you not to discuss your testimony with the other witnesses. Thank you."

Rocco Jr. was dismissed from the hearing room and his father, Rocco Sr., admitted. Chairman Walsh administered the oath and had the witness introduce himself.

"I understand you also have a prepared statement to read?"

"Yes, I do."

"Please go ahead."

"I appear before you to discuss this situation. My son, Rocco Jr., informed me that NSTAR had a contractor Vendor List and that he pursued it with NSTAR and was told that he would be placed on a waiting list. He asked me if I knew anyone or if it would be okay to contact his Uncle John? I told him that I would talk to associates and that he should contact his Uncle John because my brother knew many more people than I. Outside of the day-to-day operations and normal daily discussion of our business I personally had no other direct contacts with this situation. Thank you."

Chairman Walsh said, "Thank you for that, and if there are no other questions, I want to remind the witness not to discuss his testimony with any of the other witnesses. Thank you."

Rocky left the hearing room and joined others remaining in the corridor.

Richard F. Wright

Witness: Patricia 'Tricia' Uwazany

One of the allegations concerned the impression that Representative Fresolo was using his influence to help his sister avoid jury duty. His sister, Patricia Uwazany, is self-employed as a hairstylist and works up to six days a week in Worcester. She lives in the town of Brimfield and commutes to Worcester every day. When she received her jury duty notice, she asked her brother how she could get an assignment closer to Brimfield, where she lives, or to Worcester, where she worked. The initial request for Springfield disturbed her as it was far away and in a place, she was not familiar with at all.

Fresolo made some calls, and his aide made some calls to help Tricia find out what the procedure was to request a change of venue. Ultimately, she got a change of venue and went to her assigned jury duty day. She did not get out of reporting to the court. As it turned out, which often happens, she was not empaneled that day by the court.

Fresolo collected his sister from the holding area and escorted her into the hearing room. She took the oath from Chairman Walsh, and he started the questioning.

"Ms. Uwazany, we understand that you were called for jury duty and that you asked your brother to get you out of it."

"That's not true. I asked if he could help me move to a location closer to my home or closer to my job so that it would not be such an inconvenience."

"Did you tell the Representative's aide that you were afraid of going into Springfield, that it was dangerous?"

"Going into Springfield is something I don't do. I don't know the city, the roads, and anything. I prefer to do things in Worcester where I know people and the roads."

"Did Ms. Ryan help you?"

"She made a call to see if the Palmer Court was available, but she found out they didn't have jury activity, so that didn't help."

"Did you report for jury duty?"

"Yes, I went to the courthouse, and on the day I went in they didn't need any jurors, so those who went in were sent home. It stills counts for reporting."

"Do any members have more questions?"

Hearing no questions, Walsh thanked her and reminded her not to share her testimony with the other witnesses.

Witness: George and Matthew Panagiotou

An allegation had been made that Representative Fresolo was securing tickets for events at the TD Garden in Boston and improperly overcharging the face value of the tickets. For the most part, except for some tickets he purchased for himself, it was his two friends, two brothers, George and Matthew Panagiotou that the Representative bought tickets for. In all cases, the brothers paid the face value, and whatever handling charge was included in the price that Representative Fresolo incurred and no more.

George Panagiotou and brother Matthew were lifelong friends of John and had also grown up as Yankee supporters in New England, the two brothers, who were Greek, would always kid John when he spoke to them in Greek.

"Hey, John, are you really Greek or not?"

When Fresolo called George to ask him to testify, he said he would be happy to do it. He and his brother set aside their personal and work schedule to be available in Boston at 9:00 AM as they had been instructed. When they got to the State House, the guard did not know who they were or why they were asking to park. After some explanations, the guard directed them to a parking area and told them what entrance to use at the back of the building.

The brothers made their way inside and eventually found the waiting area for witnesses. They joined the group that had already arrived.

Later, in the afternoon, when it was their turn, Fresolo came into the waiting area and called for George to come into the hearing room.

Chairman Walsh acknowledged George Panagiotou, when he was escorted into the hearing room, asked him his name and address, and proceeded to swear him in.

Walsh addressed the witness, "Mr. Panagiotou, can you tell us about how Representative Fresolo helped you get tickets to events at the TD Garden?"

"Sure. John would get the tickets, and I would pay for them."

"I understand that Mr. Panagiotou, but can you tell me how he got the tickets to you?"

"He would either drop them off, or I would pick them up."

"Well, I'm looking to understand how he paid for them and how you paid him for the tickets?"

"I think he paid with his debit card and then I would pay him in cash when I saw him. In one case, for a concert there were two tickets, each was $220, so he bought them, and I paid him the $440 for the two tickets. It was an Eagles concert, and I remember saying to my son – you better appreciate this birthday present!"

"Can you tell us why you asked Representative Fresolo to get the tickets for you?"

"Well, it's simple, he might get better seats or something like that. Anyone can call over and get tickets, the price is the same, but maybe if it's sold out or near sold out, they can find some."

"How many times has he bought tickets for you?"

"Well, he got the Eagles tickets, and there was another group, the Foo-Foos, or Pho-Foos?"

"Do you mean the Foo Fighters?"

Some laughter among the committee members.

"Yes, that's it – I don't know these groups – but yes, the Foo Fighters tickets."

"There was one other time, John got tickets to the NCAA games but couldn't go, so he asked if I wanted them? It was an odd price like $101 for a ticket, so it was $202 for the pair of tickets. I said sure, and we bought those. I'm not sure why they have the odd price."

"Alright, Mr. Panagiotou, that will be all. I would remind you as we mentioned to you earlier that we request you not discuss your testimony with the other witnesses. Thank you."

To a more or less same degree, when it was his turn, Matthew Panagiotou gave the same testimony as did his brother regarding his relationship with Fresolo and the few occasions where he obtained tickets for an event at the TD Garden. The interview with Matthew was as brief as the interview with his brother George had been.

Witness: Dan Cahill, a former aide

A former aide to Fresolo, Dan Cahill, was called as a witness to confirm that Fresolo was not a computer savant. Not that sworn testimony was necessary, but Fresolo wanted everyone to understand that he didn't interact on the House computer and never had. Dan would testify that he didn't.

Cahill served as Fresolo's aide and began studying law at the same time. He eventually became a lawyer, and later he served on the Lynn City Council and finally ran for a seat as a State Representative for the City of Lynn.

"Mr. Chairman, I have asked Dan Cahill to testify as you know he previously served as an aide to me. Dan can comment on what he knows about my familiarity with the Internet and Facebook, and for that matter, most anything to do with email or other technology."

Fresolo escorted Cahill to the witness table, and Chairman Walsh administered the oath.

Walsh said, "I want to thank Mr. Cahill for taking the time to appear before this hearing. What can you tell us about Representative Fresolo's familiarity with the State House email system, the use of passwords, and the use of Facebook?"

"Mr. Chairman, I served as an aide for Representative Fresolo at a time when we were all learning about email and such things as Facebook. At first, these social media programs were not well understood or used by a lot of elected officials. But, as time went by, it was obvious that some officials were finding it a helpful way to reach certain constituencies. I helped him get his name out through Facebook."

"What was the purpose of that?"

"It was a way to quickly put a message to our supporters. Anyone that John friended would be able to see his activities, appearing at functions, meeting with officials, attending meetings, especially in the community."

"Did the Representative actively use social media?"

"Actually, and let me apologize here to the Rep., (Cahill turned to face Fresolo at his table) - let's face it, boss, you really weren't a tech guy and didn't know how to use social media – I would take things he wanted to send out and do it for him. I had the passwords to email, and I would transmit what he wanted. It wasn't something he knew how to do. He was a phone guy, he didn't use the computer, he just used his phone constantly."

"Mr. Cahill, can you tell us what Representative Fresolo was like to work for?"

Cahill said, "He was a good boss. He was active in cooperating with other Reps to get funding for Worcester-based projects. He would co-sponsor a lot of issues to secure funding for needs in his district."

The committee had no further questions for Cahill, so Chairman Walsh thanked him and reminded him not to discuss his testimony with the other witnesses. Walsh then dismissed him.

Witness: Sheila Trapasso

Attorney Kiley had told Fresolo that Sheila's testimony was important not so much for its details about how campaign volunteers worked on the campaign as it was to demonstrate the contradictions he felt were so prevalent in Ryan's accusations, interview comments, and testimony at the hearing. Contradictory testimony on any one topic would reflect on the other allegations made by Ryan as well.

Sheila Trapasso was a witness for Fresolo regarding one of the most sensitive of the accusations against him, which was that he forced his aide to work on campaign-related activities including attending and running fundraising functions in his district. While it's not appropriate to force an employee of the state to work on a candidate's campaign, there is no prohibition against an employee volunteering to help outside of paid working hours. Fresolo had maintained that Ryan had done some campaign work, but he had not made it a job requirement or done during work hours.

Sheila was a longtime volunteer on Fresolo's campaign stretching back to his very first election. As time passed, she emerged as his campaign manager, and not just as a figurehead manager, but as the actual roll-up-your sleeves headmaster of a group of volunteers that came together every two years to help re-elect the Representative. His most recent election was a relatively easy one compared to others in years past as he had no real competition as he sought his eighth term in office.

Sheila and Fresolo had married each other's spouse's cousins. They had both grown up in the same part of Worcester in and about Grafton Hill and Union Hill, so it was no surprise that she became involved in his campaign. Her father had been an active community leader, and when he retired as a firefighter in the City of Worcester, he became even more active. Sheila was raised in a family that felt it was everyone's duty to give back to the community and serving as an elected official was an important part of that belief. Sheila's Dad had run for office himself, although he was never victorious, he felt he had the chance to contribute by how he and his family engaged fully in the election process. Sheila was well acquainted with politics and politicking. She stuffed a lot of envelopes over the years for friends of her Dad.

Sheila recalled when the current City Manager of Worcester, Eddy Augustus was 22 years old, he was at the house campaigning for school committee. Other candidates for local offices, such as Guy Glodis, would be at the house as he ran for State Representative. To Sheila, all of this was fascinating and exciting. So, when Fresolo looked around for someone to take over as manager, his cousin Larry suggested his wife, Sheila, would be ideal. Everyone agreed, and Sheila had been involved ever since.

Now, her childhood-chum, family-member was under fire. Wild accusations had been hurled at him, and Sheila could not understand how this could be happening. Fresolo had called her to explain that his aide was making accusations against him and that he wanted her to testify in response to the allegation that he forced his aide to work on his campaign. She listened as Fresolo explained that she was the best witness to refute the allegation and that he felt she would be the most helpful in explaining that Ryan was not involved in his campaign activities.

For Sheila, it was ludicrous for Ryan to claim she worked on the campaign. Almost five or six nights a week during an active campaign season, Sheila and her friends and campaign volunteers worked on Fresolo's campaign doing all the things all candidates need to do. They made countless phone calls, including polling calls, they wrote out invitations and envelopes for fundraisers, for rally's and for coffee parties or picnics. When someone donated, Fresolo wrote a personal note, and the volunteers wrote out envelopes and stamped them.

In the two years that Ryan had been an aide to the Representative, Sheila had seen her only once in Worcester. It was at the PNI event, and she recalled clearly that when Ryan offered to sit at the Welcome Desk at the event, Sheila had to firmly request that Ryan not be at the front of the hall as it was not allowed. She had volunteered, which was nice, but the experienced campaign manager knew it was not permitted. How could anyone believe that Ryan was "working" on the campaign?

Sheila immediately responded to the Representative that she would be happy to testify as to how the campaign conducted its business and that Ryan was not a part of any campaign activities.

Just before the hearing date, Sheila received another call from Fresolo asking for some added help.

"Sheila, would you be willing to drive my two daughters into Boston on Friday when you come in to testify? Both of them will be testifying too. They are nervous about driving to Boston, finding someplace to park, because Chairman Walsh had not provided parking passes yet, and they are not sure what they are expected to do. The hearing starts at 9:00 AM, so you might expect that you will be there for a few hours and then you can take them home. I will have to stay much longer, and I don't want them to have to wait so long."

Sheila immediately agreed to bring the girls with her. She had been notified that she should be on hand and ready to testify at 9:00 AM on Friday, May 17, 2013, at the Hearing Room in the State House. To allow for traffic, Sheila wanted to leave Worcester no later than 7:00 AM, which meant she had to pick up the two girls before that. Already, she could see it would be a long day.

It was time for Sheila to enter the hearing room. Fresolo addressed the Chairman.

"Mr. Chairman, my next witness is Sheila Trapasso. She will testify in rebuttal to the allegation that I forced my aide to work on my campaign."

Fresolo rose and walked around the end of the Committee's bench and out into the corridor where all of the witnesses were standing. Fresolo took Sheila by the arm and escorted her toward the door. He turned to his two daughters, who had been standing with Sheila.

"Girls, you will be next after Sheila. I will come out and get you."

Each of Fresolo's daughters had been keeping close to Sheila since arriving at the State House at about 8:00 AM. After sitting in the waiting room from 9:00 AM until about 3:00 PM, except for the meal break, they had been standing with the others in the corridor for two hours. The only one who was sitting in the corridor was retired Representative Rucho. After he had been called in and finished his testimony, he returned to wait with the rest of the witnesses.

Sheila and the Representative entered the hearing room, and Sheila was shown to her seat. Immediately, Chairman Walsh asked, "Please state your name?"

"Sheila Trapasso."

Walsh administered the oath, but before he could ask a question, Representative Patricia Haddad (D-5th Bristol District) spoke up.

"As I understand it, said Haddad, "Jamie Ryan ran all of the Representative's fundraising events, is that so?"

"Well, actually that's a bald-faced lie. She never ran anything, ever. Anyone who says she worked on the campaign is a liar."

"What did she do?"

"She did nothing. We ran John's campaign. We meet as an informal group to prepare mailings, to make phone calls, to organize where we will install lawn signs, and occasionally make polling phone calls. We have been doing this for all of John's campaigns for the past 16 years. Jamie has only worked for John these past two years and has only been to Worcester once that I remember."

"Did she work on invitations?"

"That's a lie. We do invitations. We handwrite envelopes for invitations, and sometimes we have labels printed from John's list of supporters that we affix to the envelopes. We only do two fundraisers a year, and they are planned well in advance, so it's no trouble to get the work done with our usual volunteers."

"Did she work at the fundraiser in Worcester?"

"No, she did not. In fact, the one event she did attend, she did come to the Welcome Desk at the front of the hall where we sign people in and asked if she could help. I told her we were all set and in fact, I went on to tell her that she should wait in the back of the hall as she was not supposed to be at the table with us. So, she went back."

"How do you get the names you are inviting?"

"I'm not sure what you mean?"

"Where do names come from?"

"These are John's supporters. People that contribute, people who volunteer to stand at the polls, or to host a coffee party. They are on the list. After they come to one of the fundraisers, we invite them every year. It's the same group year after year. We know who they all are. They are his supporters."

"Who prints the invitations?"

"I don't know who prints them. John brings them to us, and we stuff the envelopes and put on the stamps."

"Where do you do this?"

"We do it at our houses, or John's, or once in a while for certain campaigns in the past, we have had a headquarters where we can store signs and recruit volunteers and hold meetings. One year it was in a small plaza on Grafton Street."

Chairman Walsh interjected, "Does anyone else have any other questions?"

Turning to Sheila, Walsh thanked her, and Sheila got up from the table to leave.

Suddenly, Representative Shaunna O'Connell called out to Sheila, "Where do you get the lists?"

"I'm sorry?"

Sheila turned back to the table and again took a seat. She said, "What was it?"

"Where did you get the lists?"

"I'm not sure what you mean. The list is the list of John's supporters. He's had the list for years, and we add names and subtract names."

There were no further questions, so Sheila got up again from the table, and Fresolo escorted her out to the corridor. Here he took his daughter Frankie into tow. The two girls approached Sheila and asked what happened.

"Girls, it's fine. They just ask questions about what you know, and you just answer them. It'll be fine. They have a long table and a lot of people sitting there. They will ask you some questions. I'll be waiting for you here when you are done. We can leave then."

The John Fresolo Saga

Witness: Francesca 'Frankie' Fresolo

John led his daughter into the hearing room. Frankie took a seat at the table, and Chairman Walsh swore her in.

Fresolo was visibly upset about seeing his daughter sitting alone at the witness table with the 11 member ethics committee hovering over her. She had been brave when he asked if she thought she could testify, but he knew she and her sister were both feeling anxious and unsure of themselves. What if they made a mistake?

He had tried to assure them not to worry. The committee wanted to know some things that they could recall, and he had told them they had done nothing wrong. They couldn't hurt him or themselves. For John, it was easier to let them drive the family car the first time than to go through this.

It was Representative Shaunna O'Connell (D-Taunton) who asked a question instead of the Chairman.

"Ms. Fresolo, can you tell us about the help you got from Ms. Ryan with your resume?"

"My father said that she would help me put it together and she did."

"Why didn't you have someone in your family help you with the resume?"

"Well, if I had, my mother would have done a better job."

Fresolo interrupted the questioning.

"Excuse me, Representative, it was just an issue of timing. It was something that had to be done quickly, and my aide could do it immediately, it would have taken too long; otherwise, that's all."

Chairman Walsh asked if anyone else had a question and hearing none he thanked her for coming in and dismissed her.

Fresolo got up from his table and walked his daughter out of the room. When he got outside, he took his other daughter, Maria by the arm and led her into the room.

Witness: Maria Fresolo

Maria took a seat at the witness table, and Chairman Walsh had her give her name and take the oath.

The questions were few, and it turned out that Fresolo's aide had made a few phone calls for the Representative to set up appointments and gather information about her attending college.

None of the committee members had any real interest in further questioning.

Chairman Walsh thanked Maria for coming in, reminded her not to share her testimony with other witnesses, and dismissed her.

Fresolo rose and walked his daughter out to the corridor where the witnesses were still standing around.

Witness: Officer Ruffin and Officer Hinkley

Fresolo returned to the hearing room and addressed the Chairman.

"Mr. Chairman, we have two final witnesses, both of whom are court officers and are on duty today. They are here now and are available to testify now."

Chairman Walsh said, "Let's have them come in." He directed that each officer be brought in one at a time.

Chairman Walsh then indicated to admit Officer Hinkley. He administered the oath and addressed the witness.

"Thank you, Officer Hinkley, for coming in today. You have the floor."

"Thank you, Mr. Chairman. I guess that you are asking about the Rep and being in the building. I would say I saw the Rep as much as I saw anybody. He was there every day. He's a Yankee fan, as you probably know, and being a Red Sox fan, we would needle each other every day, especially if the Red Sox beat the Yankees or they were ahead in the standings."

"How is it you saw him so often?"

"I'm at my desk outside the House Chamber, and the Rep is on the third floor a lot, so he stops and talks."

Committee member Representative Matthew Beaton (R-Shrewsbury), who had commented earlier about evidence about Representative Fresolo's attendance, spoke up and asked a question.

"Officer Hinkley, have you ever seen the Representative in informal attire – like golf shirts?"

"Actually, quite often. Representative Fresolo always wears nice slacks and polo shirts and is quite well dressed. He wears suits on formal session days like everyone else, but on other days he is still well dressed, but casual."

With that answer, Chairman Walsh asked if there were any more questions, and hearing none, he thanked Officer Hinkley and addressed him.

"Please remember not to discuss your testimony with the other witnesses. Thank you."

The next to come in was Odell Ruffin, a longtime court officer, and someone who had a cordial relationship with Representative Fresolo over the years.

Chairman Walsh administered the oath and addressed the witness.

"Officer Ruffin, thank you for coming today. We hope this will be brief for you."

"Thank you, Mr. Chairman."

"Officer Ruffin, would you please tell us what you have observed about Representative Fresolo's attendance?"

"Yes, sir. I have known the Rep for a long time, and he and I are friendly. He visits with me and Officer Hinkley on the third floor frequently."

"Can you describe when you see him?"

"We see him all the time."

"Specifically, do you see him on days that are full formal session and days that are not full session?"

"Yes, sure. The Rep comes in and talks to us very often. He is there more than most other Reps that we see."

"Have you seen Representative Fresolo in casual clothes in the building?"

"We do see him in casual clothes, he wears dressed-up casual clothes, nothing sloppy."

"Fine, Officer Ruffin. Thank you. I want to remind you not to discuss your testimony with the other witnesses."

Today was a Friday, and despite the implied formality of a secret hearing in the State House, Chairman Walsh had been in shirtsleeves all day. It was Friday.

The hour was late; it had been a long day with the final state witness in the morning and the entire group of defense witnesses in the afternoon.

Chairman Walsh noted the time as being late in the afternoon and expressed satisfaction that all the witnesses had been heard, which was not true. Representative Binienda, who had been subpoenaed and had been in the State House throughout the day was not brought in to testify on the matter of per diems, which was the issue that Fresolo had asked him to clarify for the committee.

As Fresolo was addressing his attorney to understand the status of Binienda's appearance, Chairman Walsh addressed Fresolo.

"John, are you prepared to make a statement on your behalf to the committee?"

"Yes, Mr. Chairman, I do have a statement that I want to make."

Fresolo pulled the folders together on his desk and withdrew the typed and hand-written document he had prepared for his closing remarks. He was concerned that Binienda had not been called and his Attorney seemed not to be reacting to this. The room sensed that they were giving John his last opportunity to make his case on the various allegations.

Richard F. Wright

Fresolo Closing Statement

"Mr. Chairman, I have learned a lot over these three days. One of the things that stunned me is how much information there is out there on each of us in this technological age. Big brother really is watching us, and there is good and bad in that. Whether the good outweighs the bad is a matter for another day.

What I want you to understand is that I am a dinosaur concerning this technology. None of the things you have before you concerning my per diems – the things Mr. Frongillo described as "circumstantial evidence," were part of what I used when I filled out my annual certification on per diem allowance. I'm old school, not a "high tech" guy, and I'm also not a lawyer. From the perspective of a non-lawyer, rather, a lawmaker, I would think that when that circumstantial evidence conflicts, as my EZ Pass records conflict with the information you have from my cell phone, the tie would always go to the runner. All the more so when only a little piece of the technology, not cameras and the like, is used.

What I did employed none of this technology. I managed on a paper calendar. Here's the one I currently use. (John held up the calendar in his hand.) It's in my office every day, and none of the witnesses against me have alluded to it at all. And I'd ask questions. I'd ask John Binienda and the people we came in with what they remembered, and I'd ask my aides, like Dan Cahill, and Paul McClory, what they had. Testimony was given by State House employees and a former Rep that rode in with me daily, that I was in Boston on days Mr.

Frongillo claims I was not. His evidence is corrupted phone and EZ pass data.

When Annie (Martin-McDonough) came to work for me, in her short six-week stint, there was no occasion for it to have happened with her to file a per diem report as she did not work for me when I put in my request for the time she was there, despite her statement to House Counsel to the contrary.

Are there mistakes in it? Today I can say yes, but then I could not. That is because I learned something different about the statute that I did not know before. Mr. Frongillo brought to your attention a day when the records before you indicated I was in Somerville and Medford and suggested if I didn't come to the State House that day, I was not entitled to a per diem payment for it. I never understood things that way. When I came into Quincy to pick things up for my constituents at the Registry, I would have considered that a per diem day. If I traveled to Methuen or Amherst for a legislative committee meeting, I would have considered that a per diem day.

I'm not telling you I remember being in Somerville and Medford on a given day, but I told you I would tell the truth and the truth is if I were here or anywhere on what I thought to be legislative business, I would have put in for it. I am sorry I was wrong but never intended to be wrong. If these proceedings weren't pending, if someone had said something to me, I would have already adjusted.

I have tried to address the list of allegations that have been made against me. The witnesses have testified to clarify misstatements and false allegations. I am asking the committee to understand that despite the sensational headlines, the issue with personal messages and a graphic photograph should not be an issue for the ethics committee to consider. These were personal, person-to-person communications, that accidentally got into the state system. Any instant messages I wrote were intended to be read by a person who was expecting such messages.

I hope everyone is clear on the fact that I never intended to harass someone, rather, that I was engaged in a personal person-to-person conversation that was private and was intended to be kept private. My aide finding it was a surprise to me, to her, to IT, and everyone else. We should all now be on notice of how phone texts can end up flowing through the House system.

The testimony of the complainant has debunked the allegation of a no-show job herself. Despite numerous declarations that she never spoke to or saw Mr. Simoncini, she contradicted herself completely by acknowledging that she discussed holiday vacation schedules, met him at a district event, made parking arrangements for him, helped with scheduling for training sessions, sought his advice for constituents on tax matters, and more. Further, local community activists in my district have testified that Mr. Simoncini was someone they dealt with regularly and satisfactorily. The interpretation must be that Mr. Simoncini worked for me and did his job as directed by me. If pay slips are missing, it's clear that Human Resources has not yet been able to show that anyone else is fulfilling this requirement correctly either.

Finally, just like most of you, I have been serving my district aggressively for many years. As a poorer urban area, there tend to be more constituent services toward helping people find a good job rather than filing college tuition reimbursement legislation. And, if my family members ask for the same kind of help, to cut some red tape, should I turn my back on them?

The testimony you heard shows that sometimes people ask for things that maybe they should handle themselves. But, I am inclined to be helpful, and I don't think you would want me to do less. No one benefitted beyond getting strong moral support to file an application, request a change of venue, or be placed on the vendor list. I received no benefit from this assistance, and in the case of family members, I already had their vote.

My Attorney has expressed to you through the Chairman my willingness to repay any per diem that falls outside of the committee's interpretation as valid. I would expect that such a courtesy would be extended to any other member who had made some errors in their filings.

Thank you for your attention."

With that, Fresolo concluded his statement. He thought to himself that he hoped his reference to "any other member," was not so subtle that the committee missed the reference to Representative Binienda. The so-called third most powerful man in the State House routinely filed for more per diem days each year than John, so he may owe a few days back too.

Richard F. Wright

Chapter Seven

Motion for Settlement

Evening of Friday, May 17, 2013

Chairman Walsh was sorting his notes, and Attorney Frongillo was trying to whisper something to him when a voice broke through the low chatter in the room. Fresolo had just finished his closing statement, and the committee was waiting for Walsh to wrap things up.

Instead, it was Representative Theodore Spiliotis (D-Danvers) who spoke up.

"Mr. Chairman, can I make a motion that you, Mr. Chairman, and Representative Fresolo and his Attorney go out in the hallway and try to come to some resolution, some common ground that we can all agree on, and then we can end this nightmare for John and his family?"

Chairman Walsh said, "Does anybody have an objection to that?"

No one objected, and the three men proceeded to leave the hearing room and moved to the outside corridor just outside the House Counsel office.

Fresolo was immediately buoyed by this motion. As he glided out the door into the hallway, he envisioned that the committee members had quietly determined that a compromise on how to resolve the allegations was within reach.

Immediately, Chairman Walsh saw the opportunity to get a resolution that would allow the committee to make a recommendation and get agreement from Fresolo so that both sides could survive the ordeal. He turned to Fresolo's Attorney and said, "Tom, what would you suggest as reasonable for the committee to consider as a resolution?"

Kiley jumped right in. He had discussed just this sort of scenario with Fresolo previously that they needed to be prepared to offer or accept a compromise.

"We would agree that John is not allowed to file claims for per diem for the remainder of his current term. We would also agree that on the dates where the committee had indicated they had questions on previous claims, we would acknowledge them and pay back the amount overclaimed. We would ask perhaps for a time-payment be considered in that event, but we would pay back what they felt was owed."

Fresolo was a bit taken aback at the bold statement about per diems. But, he realized his Attorney wanted to bring a strong response to the Chairman so that it would find acceptance with the committee.

Chairman Walsh immediately said, "Well, that certainly sounds reasonable, it sounds more than fair, let me check with the committee to see how they find it. It may be something they would accept."

Fresolo also recognized at that moment that his Attorney was willing to accept chastisement about per diems and no one was any longer worried about someone sending lurid photos to unwanted viewers. The committee had long since dropped its concern with that.

While Walsh went back inside the hearing room, Fresolo and Kiley stood quietly listening to the muffled conversation taking place behind the wall. They couldn't hear the words, but someone was a bit more forceful than the others.

Walsh came back out and said that the committee wanted something more.

"Do you have anything else?"

Kiley responded, "What are they looking for, are they giving any suggestions?"

Chairman Walsh said, alright I'll go back in and see what they want."

After a while, Walsh emerged again from the hearing room.

"They haven't reached a consensus yet, but they are still considering what they want. I'm just here to give you an update that they are trying."

Walsh went back in, and on this third attempt, he was in the hearing room a bit longer.

Fresolo could now determine that it was Representative Kathi-Anne Reinstein's voice that he could hear. He couldn't hear what she was saying, but she was apparently dominating the conversation. Reinstein had been elected the same year as Fresolo. She was a "classmate," someone who came to the

State House in the same class. She was elected Co-President of their class. John felt his relationship with her was good, but just like the fallout he had with Binienda, she sided with DeLeo and Fresolo had backed Rogers for Speaker. At that point, a wall went up between him and Reinstein. She was entrenched in Leadership.

Fresolo and Kiley continued to wait for Chairman Walsh to reemerge.

Out of the corner of his eye, Fresolo saw Walsh and Attorney Frongillo slip out the other door of the hearing room and head for the elevator.

Kiley saw it at the same time.

"You know where those two are going, don't you?"

Fresolo knew. It was very late on Friday night. The State House was virtually cleared out. The men's room is on this floor. The only reason those two went into the elevator was to go up two more flights to the Speaker's office.

Kiley continued, "They may have something they have agreed to and want to get the Speaker's okay."

Fresolo tried to keep his emotions in check. His whole life was about to be pushed across the desk of the Speaker, and any outcome tonight would be as a result of the committee reaching an agreement that would meet everyone's approval.

The elevator door opened, and someone came out. They approached Fresolo and Kiley.

"We're not going to have this tonight. Better go home. We'll meet on Monday morning."

That was it.

It wasn't what John expected or wanted, but, even though it meant another few days delay, the hearing was over, the evidence and rebuttal were done, and now the committee could make its determination on how much punishment they wanted to deal out to John.

Fresolo had endured three consecutive days of secret testimony all relating to 13 allegations of unethical behavior brought to the Office of Legal Counsel for the House of Representatives to consider. After the testimony concluded, a motion put forward by Representative Spiliotis was accepted by the committee. Terms of the settlement had been offered and modified during a brisk series of exchanges outside the hearing room. A postponement to Monday had been enforced by the Chairman as it had been decided it would not get finished that evening.

Richard F. Wright

Part Three - Conspiracy

con-spir-a-cy

noun

- a secret plan by a group to do something unlawful or harmful; the action of plotting

Richard F. Wright

Chapter Eight

Final Session Executive Conference

Saturday, May 18, 2013

John Fresolo woke after a fitful night of toss and turn sleep. It had been 65 days since Jamie Ryan handed a photograph of his genitals to Fleming; sixty-five days since his life went into a tailspin.

For two months he had been fighting to keep his head above water. He was as a drowning man contemplating whether it was better to struggle or submit. Would letting go let the dying be easier? No. Fresolo was not one to submit. He cut his political teeth on bringing the message of his neighbors to the State House, and they had just said resoundingly only a few months ago that they wanted to have his voice speak for them on Beacon Hill. Didn't his polling show he could run for Senate and be successful? Not that he wanted to do that, but it meant a lot that he knew he could run with reasonable assurance of success. Not easy in politics to feel that sure.

The sweat poured down on his brow from his morning workout. He tried to keep fit. He never drank alcohol. He prided himself as always being presentable and approachable whether at work in the State House or at the grocery store on Grafton Hill. He had made some mistakes along the way. He knew that. He tried to be right-thinking in everything he did, but sometimes the pressures got to him.

His routine today would be similar to every other day. He would call Billy on the phone. He would call Sheila on the phone. He might even call Ray or Franny. He had to let them know that the ethics committee had come close to closing on a settlement last night and he was optimistic that an acceptable agreement would be finalized when they met on Monday morning. The official hearing was over. All the evidence and testimony was in. We had reached the settlement phase.

Hadn't Representative Speliotis' motion that he and Kiley caucus with Walsh to come up with a settlement, set things up for a quick solution? We almost had it, but we ran out of time. Sure, we saw Walsh and Frongillo go up the elevator, and as Kiley had said, they would look for approval on the terms they would offer to John. That made sense.

He decided to call everyone. His brother, nephew, sister, everyone. He certainly wanted to thank them for coming into Boston and spending all day waiting to give their supportive testimony. No one person's testimony could fix things, but the fact that he had 14 people drive into Boston, wait for hours all day, and then subject themselves to questioning from 11 committee members was some evidence that he was a worthy person? Right?

The phone rang. It was Sheila. Of course, I'm alright. Yes, we met for a long time after all the witnesses went home and we're in the middle of coming to an agreement. That's good to hear. Yes, I'm optimistic. I'll call back later.

He had called his daughters last night while driving home. He wanted them both to know that they had been very helpful, and he was grateful to them. He told them that he would call them again on Saturday. He thought he would wait on that as it was still kind of early.

The hearings were a blur. He remembered that he cursed himself for shouting out and being told he was out of order, with Walsh banging his gavel. He shouldn't have let that happen. But, he couldn't stand to listen to the lies and misinformation. He didn't like to see the State's attorney, Frongillo, try to intimidate Representative Beaton when he pointed out that the message was absolutely a text and not an email.

Hadn't Beaton said, "I'm not Steve Jobs or Bill Gates, but I know enough about computers to tell the difference between a text and an email."

That's what the IT guy had told John. John shouted out, "Yeah, that's right, that's what the guy from IT told me. It's a text!"

That put Frongillo in his place, didn't it? There he was screwing up his face, shaking his head, trying to squash Beaton's comments.

"He's trying to make him stop talking, Mr. Chairman," shouted Fresolo. Maybe he shouldn't have done that either.

Monday, May 20, 2013

The weather broke partly cloudy early on Monday, May 20, 2013, and cleared up by noontime with temperatures reaching 80 degrees in some places. It was a beautiful day in May.

Fresolo had spent the weekend anticipating how to maintain a calm demeanor as he negotiated the best terms possible from the settlement he was expecting with the House Committee on Ethics.

Over the weekend, the committee's counsel had notified Fresolo's attorney, Tom Kiley, that they would convene on Monday morning in the hearing room on the first floor. There were no indications that they wanted to discuss anything over the weekend. They would wait until Monday.

Fresolo had done the math in his head again about per diems. Even if he lost out on 100 percent of the so-called unaccounted dates, the total repayment would not be over $15,000. It was a large sum of money, but if they agreed to a payment plan, it would not be impossible. Kiley had also offered the committee that John would not take any per diems for the rest of his term. That was also a significant amount of money. And besides, he felt that he could argue that not all of their calculations were correct and so the bill would be lower. In any event, the total amount could be a point of negotiation.

Kiley and Fresolo were first to enter the hearing room. They sat together and discussed casually what tactics to use in reaching a final agreement. Fresolo was not interested in being confrontational at this point. He would accept a reasonable censure and punishment for being an inattentive boss about timesheets and having some unaccounted per diem requests, which he was willing to pay back.

He knew the 11 committee members had long since abandoned any concerns about the instant messaging and the one photograph. It was clearly something that could have happened to anyone, and there was no evidence of any harassing behavior on his part at all. So, with that issue aside, the others were things you could compromise on, where harassment you could not. He understood and agreed with that.

Chairman Walsh came into the hearing room and approached Fresolo.

"John, can we step aside and talk for a minute?"

"Yes, Marty, sure."

Kiley watched as Walsh turned and moved toward the door.

"John, it's okay to listen, but do not agree to anything with him."

Fresolo said, "I understand."

When they got outside, Walsh turned to Fresolo.

"John, I'm not sure where this is going to go. You might want to consider that the best thing for you is to resign."

Fresolo was incredulous.

"Resign? I'm not resigning. Why should I?"

"John, I'm suggesting that it may be best for you to resign."

Fresolo could not believe what he was hearing. Didn't Walsh on Friday night leap at the first suggestion that he drop per diems and pay back what is owed? What had changed since they had started the negotiation on a resolution, as Representative Spiliotis had suggested?"

This couldn't be about the photograph as that had stopped being a point of interest for the committee. Was it Simoncini? He's been fired for two months, and the issue is moot. If they wanted to withhold from Fresolo having an aide, he could cope with that.

"Look, Marty, I'm not resigning. I didn't have more per diem claims than Binienda. I don't see you doing anything about him."

"John, I don't have Binienda in front of me."

"Well, get him in front of you."

"John, I don't have a charge against Binienda. This is about you."

"Well, then, I want you to charge him. I'm making a charge right now."

"That will have to wait for another day. Today, I only have you in front of me."

"This is not right. What's going on?"

Chairman Walsh had done all he could. It was obvious that something had changed, and he was trying to make one last maneuver that would end the investigation and keep everything undercover.

"I have to reconvene the meeting now," said Walsh. He turned and went into the hearing room.

Fresolo went back to the table and told Kiley that Walsh advised him to resign and wouldn't elaborate on why the change in attitude from Walsh.

Chairman Walsh gaveled the session to order and spoke to his legal counsel.

"Mr. Frongillo, you have the floor. Please proceed."

Frongillo stood up and began passing out a new loose-leaf binder. It was similar in appearance to the first one the committee received on April 9, but a bit slimmer.

"We have an additional exhibit to submit to the committee for review and consideration. As you know, Representative Fresolo has made a case that he is a so-called dinosaur with computers, that he is not tech-savvy."

Everyone had a copy of the binder, including Kiley and Fresolo. When John opened it up, he couldn't believe what he saw. It was page after page of copies of instant messages between him and various women. In all cases, you could read the name of the woman, and in some cases, there was a thumbnail image of the woman too.

"What the hell is this?" Fresolo could hardly breathe. There were messages, many with lurid and suggestive comments to the women and back to him from them. Page after page from weeks ago, months ago or more. These were his private messages to women he was dating or was pursuing, or otherwise was friendly with.

Fresolo realized now that this late exhibit was an attempt to embarrass him into resigning. Now that Frongillo had made this part of the record, if the committee sent the case on to the State Ethics Commission, all of this would become public and freely available to the media to spread anyway they chose. The media had shown it was ready to believe the worst in such cases.

Most of the committee members had glanced at the pages and closed the book. They sat stone-faced and silent.

"Mr. Chairman. It's clear to anyone who looks at these messages that Representative is very familiar with instant messaging. He's not the non-tech guy he portrays himself to be."

Fresolo blurted out, "That's insane. This only shows that you snooped through my messages to make a fool of me. It only takes a phone to send a message. This shows nothing about whether I am tech-savvy."

"Mr. Chairman, we have no further exhibits."

Then Chairman Walsh finally spoke.

"The Committee has concluded its review of the allegations and has taken into consideration the testimony of many witnesses regarding each allegation. The Committee has decided that it will proceed as follows:

- We will recommend that Representative John Fresolo will have all future per diem reimbursements denied for the remainder of his current term.

- We will recommend that Representative John Fresolo have no access to a state computer for two years.

- We will recommend that Representative Fresolo will not have an Administrative or Legislative Aide assigned to him for the remainder of his current term.

- We will recommend that Representative Fresolo not have an assigned parking space provided for the remainder of his term.

- We will recommend that Representative Fresolo will pay the legal expense incurred as a result of this investigation of $96,000.

- We will recommend that all investigative reports, exhibits, and other material gathered as a result of the committee's executive conference be forwarded forthwith to the attention of the State Ethics Commission for further review and determination."

Kiley and Fresolo both sat in stunned silence. They had expected to hear a suggested resolution and be allowed to negotiate to reach a final resolution. Instead, the committee dropped this new, irrelevant lurid exhibit into the record, and announced a totally draconian punishment.

Lamely, Kiley leaned over to Fresolo, "Have you got $96,000?"

"Of course not," said Fresolo.

No per diem, no computer, no aide, no parking, pay $96,000 in costs, and then the whole investigation would be relaunched into the state Ethics Commission. Thus, making all of the allegations, testimony, exhibits, and memos public, subject to scrutiny by the press.

The women whose names and photos appeared in the instant messages would be on the front page of newspapers, websites, and blogs within a day of its release.

The State Ethics Commission would have to subpoena everyone again, hold hearings, interrogate the accusers and the accused and possibly meter out the same or stronger punishment if it was inclined.

Chairman Walsh did not look up from his notes. He announced the Executive Conference was concluded and rose from his seat. Like robots, all of the committee members rose from their seats in unison. None of them had spoken or looked at Fresolo. Half walked off to the right side and the others to the left and exited the room.

Attorney Kiley called out to Chairman Walsh, "Don't we get to respond now, Mr. Chairman? Mr. Chairman?

Chairman Walsh ignored Attorney Kiley. Kiley rose from his seat. John Fresolo slumped over onto the table, holding his head in his hands.

Attorney Kiley turned to John and sat back down.

"I've never seen anything like this before in my whole life," said Kiley.

Fresolo turned to Kiley, "What about the settlement we had reached on Friday night?

Kiley shook his. He had pointed out to John on Friday that Chairman Walsh and Committee legal counsel Frongillo had taken the elevator to the Speaker's floor. He had said to John, "You know where those two are going, right?"

The two men were alone in the hearing room. Fresolo couldn't speak. He realized that the negotiated settlement he had counted on based on the conversations Friday night had been struck down. Walsh and Frongillo had gone upstairs to describe the settlement terms and had announced it would not be concluded that night. They would reconvene to continue discussions on Monday.

While the committee had been open to discussing an agreement, had bargained back and forth a few times to settle on agreed terms, none of that mattered now.

Fresolo realized that the committee knew the picture issue was a non-issue and had set it aside. He hadn't been a harasser, preying on his staff, causing huge distress and embarrassment as some had assumed. They knew that the per diem was no worse than what Binienda and others were doing and that the evidence they had was so corrupted that it wouldn't stand examination by an unbiased audience. He had agreed to pay back any per diem that could not be confirmed.

John knew that gross statements by his former aide that he had wanted her to lie were ridiculous once they confronted her and showed the committee the police reports about his daughter's accident. Hadn't all of these many hours of testimony shown that he had made some mistakes and should be held accountable but that it shouldn't rise to the punishment of his eight-term legacy as a popular politician being ripped from him?

The various negotiated items from Friday evening were gone. There would be no opportunity to accept a punishment commensurate with the offense; rather, there was to be a public release of all the charges and no release of any testimony that had caused the committee to initially seek a settlement agreement with him.

The vigorous back and forth of Friday evening, which the committee had agreed to consider was now defunct. Once Walsh and Frongillo went up in the elevator to the third floor of the State House, it all came crashing down.

Attorney Kiley and Fresolo now understood that the late submission of electronic conversations on Monday morning was the committee's way of ensuring it would be a part of the package they released to the media, the public, and the ethics commission.

The total number of messages, the packaging in loose-leaf binders, and the 11 sets of binders all indicated it was not a project anyone engaged in over the weekend. These had been researched, edited, assembled, and held in reserve all along. They were withheld to be used as a final hammer to force Fresolo into a choice between continuing to fight the charges and expose these women to public ridicule or give up.

The purpose of assembling the messages was singular: create massive embarrassment for John and the several women who received and wrote lurid comments in what they assumed were private, personal exchanges with Fresolo. Now they were potential fodder for the press, the public, and his enemies.

Until this final morning, no one had ever seen these phone messages. None of these communications was ever seen by anyone, including Jamie Ryan, although she had seen others on a Facebook page. These messages showed the photos and names of the correspondents. These were past phone records that the committee's attorneys had dug up for the express purpose of putting him on the spot. They hadn't been presented as evidence by the committee because they were just private conversations. The committee had subpoenaed Fresolo's phone records, and now they used conversations no one had ever seen to embarrass him. The committee understood that. So, why now toss out a nearly settled agreement and simply declare they would make everything public and send it to the Ethics Commission? Why now?

Fresolo knew why now. He could clearly see that whatever form of resolution that Walsh and Frongillo showed the Speaker on Friday night was not acceptable. He imagined that the binders with the lurid messages to and from women were brought up. Why hadn't it been used in the hearings? Maybe it wasn't relevant as the committee didn't feel the photo and messages were indicative of unethical or immoral behavior by the Representative. But, if you want to force a resignation, wouldn't it be useful to have it on the record and threaten to release it publicly?

Fresolo could understand that Walsh and the committee didn't want to stand up for him in this fight. That would take backbone. It's easier to go along than to try and be upright in the face of wrath from the top. Walsh had visions of being Mayor of Boston, and he needed a friendly Speaker, not an angry Speaker.

Fresolo could imagine that they were told, you have this binder with the sex stuff in it, so put it on the record and make him blink.

Wednesday, May 22, 2013

It had been 69 days since Jamie Ryan showed Fleming a photograph of John Fresolo's genitalia. Sixty-nine days later House Clerk Steven James read John's letter of resignation to a nearly empty chamber.

The letter, which was addressed to Speaker of the House, Robert DeLeo read, "I am currently unable to effectively serve my district and regretfully submit my resignation, effective immediately, hoping that a prompt special election will be held to fill the balance of my term."

John Fresolo had blinked. It was not in him to drag the innocent women he corresponded with via instant messaging through what would have been a hailstorm of lurid headlines and wild innuendo. He could imagine the lengths that newspapers would go to for the catchiest headline. No matter that the 11 committee members had virtually tossed aside the issue of whether John was a sexual harasser. It was clear that he was not. But, what he was not, was not something that sells newspapers.

Fresolo now faced the indignity of clearing out his office. Arrangements were made for him to come in the following Sunday when no one would be at the State House except security. They would let him park where the big shots parked to make it easy to drag things out the door.

John's last wish, for a quick special election, was fulfilled the day after he resigned. A special election was announced so fast they must have had the press release ready the day they dropped the sex-message binder on him.

Epilogue

John Fresolo resigned as State Representative of the 16th Worcester district rather than ignite the second round of investigations into his alleged ethical misbehavior in front of the State Ethics Commission. Unlike the Ethics Committee of the House, which had just completed its investigation, the State Ethics Commission would not indulge in the kangaroo-court style of justice he had just been subjected to by the Speaker of the House and his Leadership cronies.

Although, no matter how justly they conducted the investigation, the damage would already be done due to the public release of the preliminary and final reports of the House Office of Legal Counsel and the somewhat lurid sex-message binder, complete with juicy comments, thumbnail headshots, and names, assembled by the ethics committee.

By rule, the evidence gathered by the House committee would have been submitted to the Ethics Commission, and it would be released publicly at the same time.

The public disclosure of the photograph, the messages, and the pictures of the women that Fresolo had been communicating with, which the ethics committee added to its evidence *after* the hearings were closed, would have been even more lascivious than the initial allegations which garnered headlines espousing words such as "dirty pix, dirty pics, genitals, explicit photos," and more. Not only would the release of the evidence be prejudicial, but it would also ensnare others in the scandal surrounding Fresolo.

Fresolo resigned abruptly once he realized how many people would be hurt by his continuing the fight. Not a quitter by nature, he was nonetheless realistic about the odds now stacked against him getting any kind of fair treatment by the House, the media, and the public.

Fresolo has not found work commensurate with his experience, education, and skillset since resigning. Even supporters of his, who have tried to help him find work, have told him that his name is toxic in the regional workplace. Six years after his resignation, a search on his name, John Fresolo, on Google, brings up a lengthy series of published articles that dwell on the accusations and the resignations, with no access to any information of an exculpatory nature for comparison.

As for Jamie Ryan, the principal complainant, she was placed on paid administrative leave once her charges were submitted to the Speaker of the House. Eventually, Ryan found herself in one of the "Speaker Special" jobs that she had feared. Less than a year later, Ryan finally left the House permanently and took a job in the private sector as an administrative aide in a non-profit agency.

The John Fresolo Saga has ended with equal shares of bitterness toward the House for John and Jamie.

Index

About the Author

Author Richard F. Wright first became involved in politics when his friend ran for School Committee – and lost. The next 40 years went better as he worked as a paid consultant for clients running for school committee, city council, sheriff, clerk of courts, county commissioner, register of probate, state representative, state senator, mayor, congressman, governor's council and governor. Wright's expertise included campaign management, public relations, and political polling.

Wright, until his retirement two years ago, had a parallel career in marketing, business management, and communications consulting for clients throughout the Northeast. He has written for newspapers, magazines, and has previously published three books. His latest effort, *The John Fresolo Saga*, is his first book about politics.

Read more about Richard F. Wright at his blog:

The Books of Richard F. Wright

http://richard-wright.blogspot.com

or at his LinkedIn site:

https://www.linkedin.com/in/richard-f-wright-jr-466a40126/

CPSIA information can be obtained
at www.ICGtesting.com
Printed in the USA
LVHW040328151019
634227LV00021B/2284/P